M A T H
Expressions
Common Core

Dr. Karen C. Fuson

GRADE

K

Volume 1

This material is based upon work supported by the
National Science Foundation
under Grant Numbers
ESI-9816320, REC-9806020, and RED-935373.

Any opinions, findings, and conclusions, or recommendations expressed in this material
are those of the author and do not necessarily reflect the views of the National Science Foundation.

VOLUME 1 CONTENTS

UNIT 1 Understand Numbers 1–10

© Houghton Mifflin Harcourt Publishing Company

***** This lesson consists only of activities from the Teacher Edition.

VOLUME 1 CONTENTS *(continued)*

© Houghton Mifflin Harcourt Publishing Company

* This lesson consists only of activities from the Teacher Edition.

* This lesson consists only of activities from the Teacher Edition.

© Houghton Mifflin Harcourt Publishing Company

VOLUME 1 CONTENTS *(continued)*

* This lesson consists only of activities from the Teacher Edition.

* This lesson consists only of activities from the Teacher Edition.

Family Letter

Dear Family:

Your child is learning math in an innovative program that weaves abstract mathematical concepts with the everyday experiences of children. This helps children understand math better.

Your child will have homework. He or she needs a **Homework Helper**. The helper may be anyone—you, an older brother or sister (or other family member), a neighbor, or a friend. Make a specific time for homework and provide your child with a quiet place to work (for example, no TV). Encourage your child to talk about what is happening in math class. If your child is having problems with math, please talk to the teacher to see how you might help.

Thank you! You are vital to your child's learning.

Sincerely,
Your child's teacher

--------✂--

Please fill out the following information and return this form to the teacher.

My child _____ will have _____
                     (child's name)   (Homework Helper's name)

as his or her Homework Helper. This person is my child's

_____.
  (relationship to child: father,
  mother, sibling, friend, etc.)

Estimada familia:

Su niño está aprendiendo matemáticas con un programa innovador que relaciona conceptos matemáticos abstractos con la experiencia diaria de los niños. Esto ayuda a los niños a entender mejor las matemáticas.

Su niño tendrá tarea y necesita a una persona que lo ayude. Esa persona puede ser usted, un hermano mayor (u otro familiar), un vecino o un amigo. Establezca una hora para la tarea y ofrezca a su niño un lugar tranquilo donde trabajar (por ejemplo un lugar sin TV). Anime a su niño a comentar lo que está aprendiendo en la clase de matemáticas. Si su niño tiene problemas con las matemáticas, por favor hable con el maestro para ver cómo usted puede ayudar.

Muchas gracias. Usted es imprescindible en el aprendizaje de su niño.

Atentamente,
El maestro de su niño

✂ -

Por favor complete la siguiente información y devuelva este formulario al maestro.

La persona que ayudará a mi niño _____ es
(nombre del niño)

_____ . Esta persona es _____
(nombre de la persona)   (relación con el niño)

de mi niño.

Introduce Number and Counting Routines

1	2	3	4	5	6
1	**2**	**3**	**4**	**5**	**6**

7	8	9	10		
7	**8**	**9**	**1**	**0**	

Number Tiles and Square-Inch Tiles **3**

Number Tiles and Square-Inch Tiles

Dear Family:

Your child has just read and discussed *Anno's Counting Book*. This book is an introduction to beginning numbers. It is filled with charming scenes that show many things all of the same number (for example, a scene showing many different groups of 3 things). Each page shows a month of the year.

We have discussed what a scene is in class. *A scene is a place where some action or event occurs, a picture*. The children will be making their own scenes or pictures. Sometimes this will be started in class and completed for homework. You can help by talking with your child about what he or she might draw, for example, your child might draw 2 of something, such as things found in a kitchen—2 plates, 2 bowls, 2 spoons.

Help your child practice counting things in daily life. Children might count how many stairs there are in your home, how many plates you need to set the table, or how many people are in the family.

Thank you for helping your child learn more about numbers and counting!

Sincerely,
Your child's teacher

COMMON CORE

Unit 1 includes the Common Core Standards for Mathematical Content for Counting and Cardinality K.CC.1, K.CC.3, K.CC.4, K.CC.4a, K.CC.4b, K.CC.4c, K.CC.5; Operations and Algebraic Thinking K.OA.1, K.OA.2, K.OA.3; Geometry K.G.2, K.G.4, K.G.6 and all Mathematical Practices.

Estimada familia:

Su niño acaba de leer y comentar un libro para contar. Este libro es una introducción a los primeros números. Está lleno de escenas fascinantes que muestran muchas cosas, todas acerca de los mismos números (por ejemplo, una escena muestra varios grupos diferentes de 3 cosas). Cada página indica un mes del año.

Hemos comentado en clase lo que es una escena. *Una escena es un lugar donde ocurre una acción o un suceso, un dibujo.* Los niños van a hacer sus propias escenas o dibujos. A veces los empezarán en clase y los terminarán de tarea. Usted puede ayudar hablando con su niño sobre lo que puede dibujar. Por ejemplo: si va a dibujar 2 de algo, podría dibujar cosas que están en la cocina, 2 platos, 2 tazones, 2 cucharas.

Ayude a su niño a practicar contando cosas que usen a diario. Los niños pueden contar cuántas escaleras hay en su casa, cuántos platos se necesitan para poner la mesa o cuántas personas hay en la familia.

¡Gracias por ayudar a su niño a aprender más sobre los números y a contar!

Atentamente,
El maestro de su niño

COMMON CORE

La Unidad 1 incluye los Common Core Standards for Mathematical Content for Counting and Cardinality K.CC.1, K.CC.3, K.CC.4, K.CC.4a, K.CC.4b, K.CC.4c, K.CC.5; Operations and Algebraic Thinking K.OA.1, K.OA.2, K.OA.3; Geometry K.G.2, K.G.4, K.G.6 and all Mathematical Practices.

Draw 5 hats.	Draw 3 cats.
Draw 4 stars.	Draw 2 cars.

Name _____

Look at what Puzzled Penguin wrote.

Help Puzzled Penguin.

6 dogs

Am I correct?

_____ dogs

Scenes and Visual Imagery

Circles

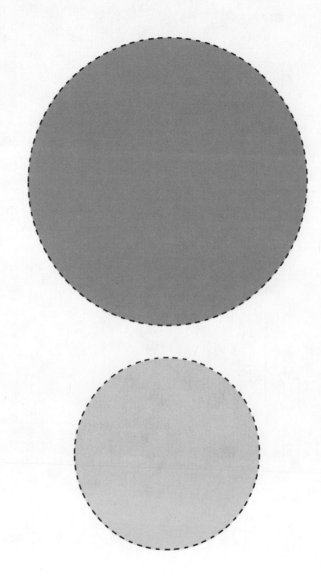

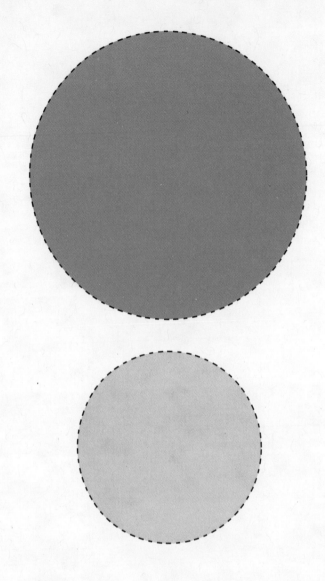

Circles

VOCABULARY
circle

Trace the **circles**.
Color the circles.

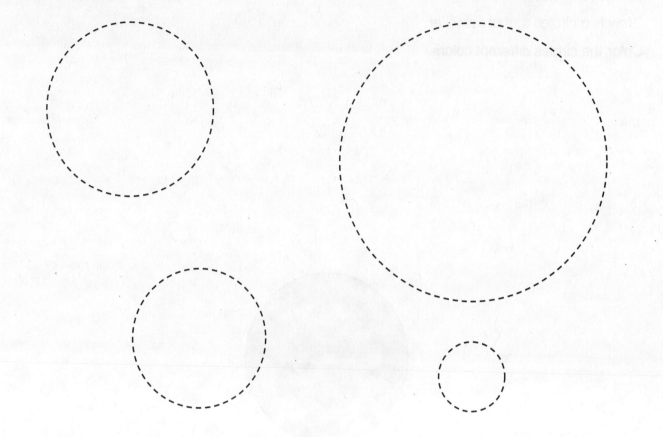

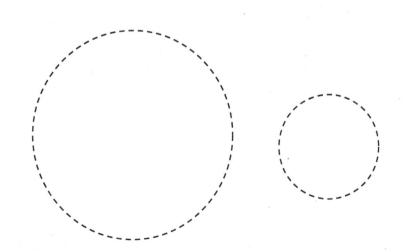

Name

Look at the red circle.

Draw two circles that are larger.

Draw two circles that are smaller.

Color the circles different colors.

Identify Circles

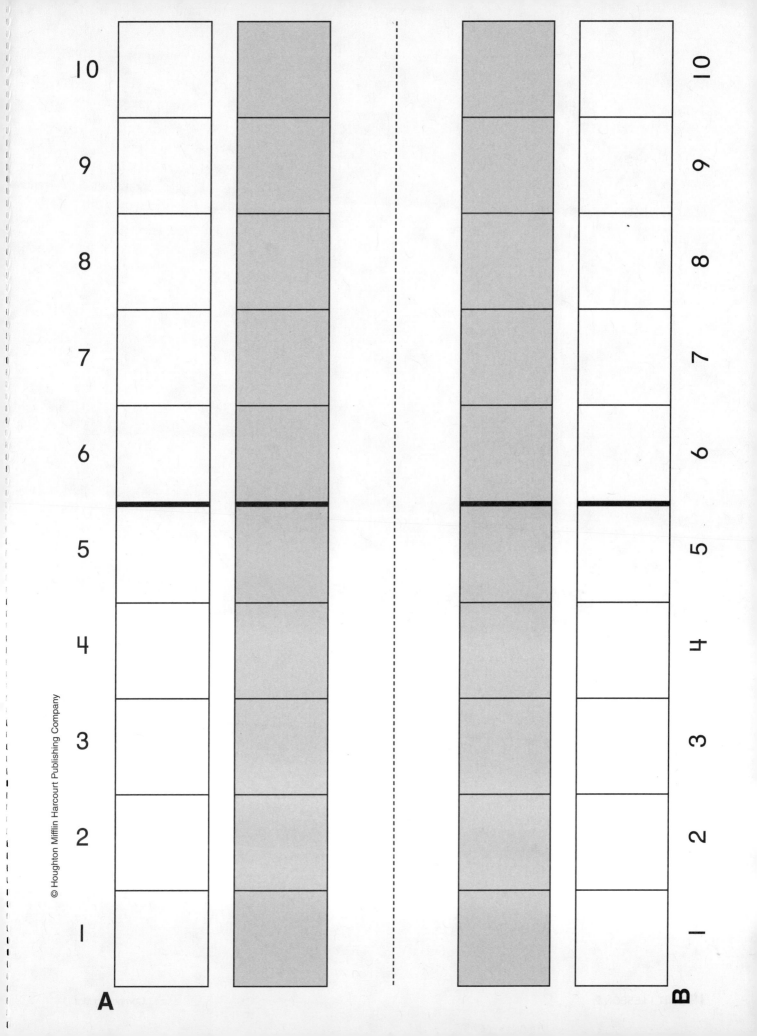

Comparing Mat

Squares and Rectangles

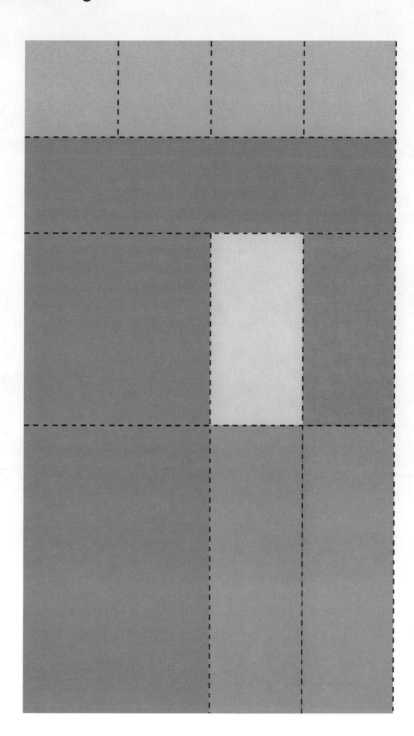

VOCABULARY
circles, squares

Color the **circles** yellow. Color the **squares** blue.
Draw a face under your favorite hat.

Name _____

VOCABULARY
circle, square,
rectangle

Color each kind of shape.

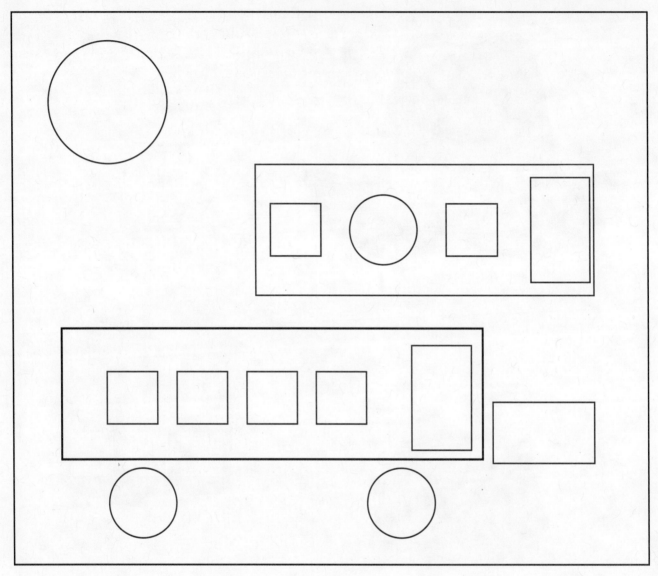

 circle

 square

 rectangle

Identify Squares and Rectangles

Dear Family:

Your child is learning to write numbers. You might notice that sometimes your child might write numbers backwards or reverse them. This is very common in early number writing. You can ask your child, "Does this number look OK?" Then point out that it is written backwards. Eventually our goal is that children may identify their own reversals, write correct numbers, and write faster in preparation for first grade.

Thank you!

Sincerely,
Your child's teacher

COMMON CORE

Unit 1 includes the Common Core Standards for Mathematical Content for Counting and Cardinality K.CC.1, K.CC.2, K.CC.3, K.CC.4, K.CC.4a, K.CC.4b, K.CC.4c, K.CC.5, K.CC.6; Operations and Algebraic Thinking K.OA.1, K.OA.2; Measurement and Data K.MD.3; Geometry K.G.1, K.G.2, K.G.3, K.G.4, K.G.5; and all Mathematical Practices.

Estimada familia:

Su niño está aprendiendo a escribir los números. Usted observará que a veces su niño escribe los números al revés o que los invierte. Esto es normal al empezar a escribir los números. Puede preguntarle, "¿Está bien escrito este número?" Luego indíquele que está escrito al revés. Nuestro objetivo es que, más adelante, los niños se den cuenta de que han invertido los números, que los escriban correctamente y que escriban más rápido para prepararse para el primer grado.

¡Gracias!

Atentamente,
El maestro de su niño

COMMON CORE La Unidad 1 incluye los Common Core Standards for Mathematical Content for Counting and Cardinality K.CC.1, K.CC.2, K.CC.3, K.CC.4, K.CC.4a, K.CC.4b, K.CC.4c, K.CC.5, K.CC.6; Operations and Algebraic Thinking K.OA.1, K.OA.2; Measurement and Data K.MD.3; Geometry K.G.1, K.G.2, K.G.3, K.G.4, K.G.5; and all Mathematical Practices.

Name _____

Write the numbers.

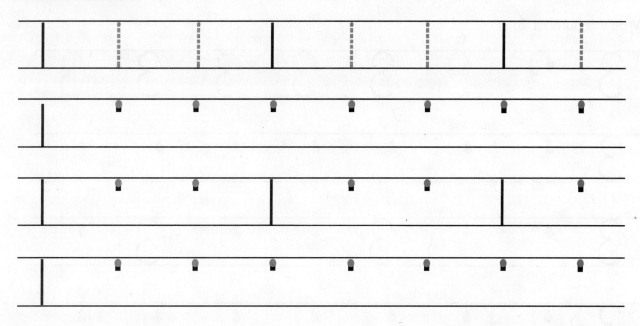

© Houghton Mifflin Harcourt Publishing Company

Name _____

VOCABULARY
circles

Write the number 3.

3 3 3 3 3 3 3 3

3

3   3   3

3

3

Draw 3 things.	Draw 3 **circles**.

© Houghton Mifflin Harcourt Publishing Company

Objects and Numbers Through 10

VOCABULARY
groups

Go left to right. Ring **groups** of the number. X out groups that are not the number.

3

4

5

2

Name _____

3 3 3 3 3 3 3

3 3 3 3 3 3 3

3 3 3 3 3 3 3

3 3 3 3 3 3 3

© Houghton Mifflin Harcourt Publishing Company

Practice Numbers I—I0

Write the number 4.

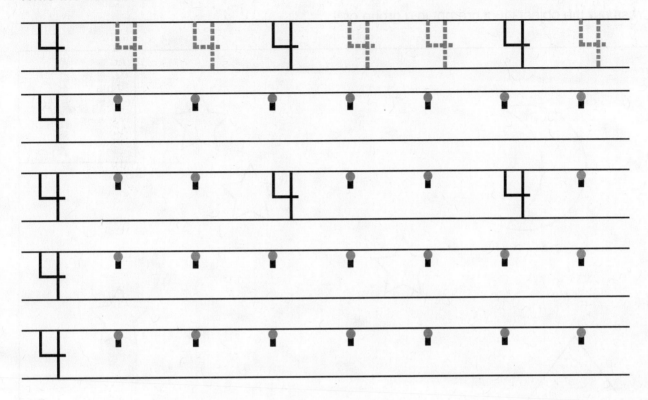

Draw 4 things.	Draw 4 rectangles.

Trace over the number 4. Color each group of 4 a different color.
Cross out the objects that are not in a group of 4.

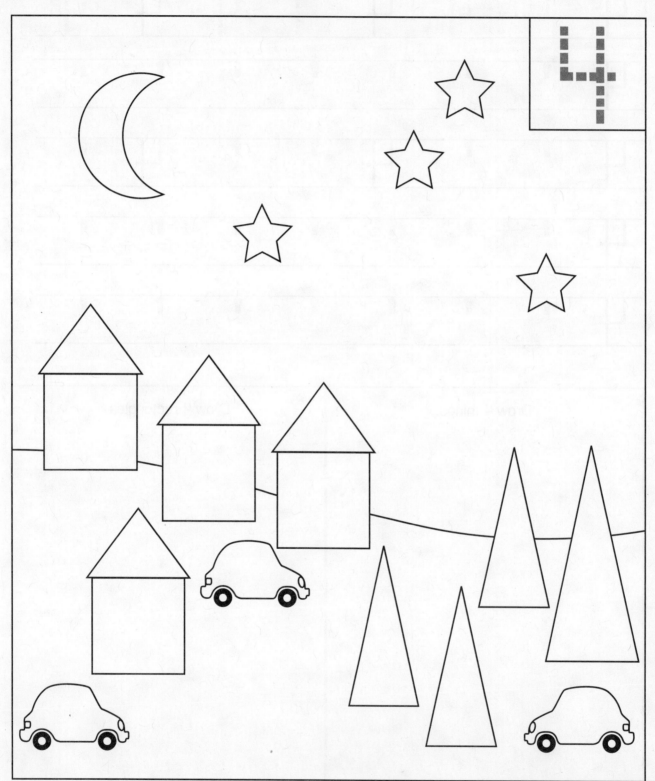

Numbers of Objects in a Group

Tell an adding story.

First	Then	At the end

1.

2.   (third panel)

Tell a subtracting story.

First	Then	At the end

3.

4.   (third panel)

Tell math stories about the pictures.

5.

6.

7.

8.

Numbers of Objects in a Group

Puzzled Penguin compared numbers.

Puzzled Penguin showed the numbers.

Then Puzzled Penguin put a circle around the number that is more. Help Puzzled Penguin.

Am I correct?

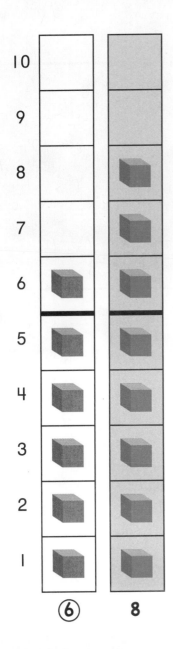

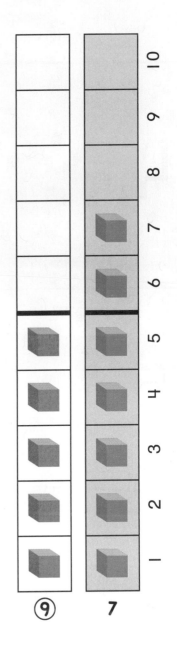

Name _____

Go left to right. Ring groups of the number. X out groups that are not the number.

3

4

5

2

Objects and Numbers Through 10

Write the number 5.

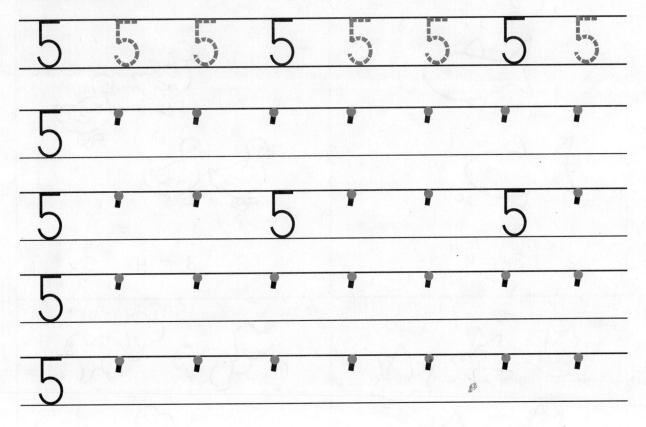

Draw 5 things.	Draw 5 squares.

Name

Count the animals. Circle the number. Then color each group a different color.

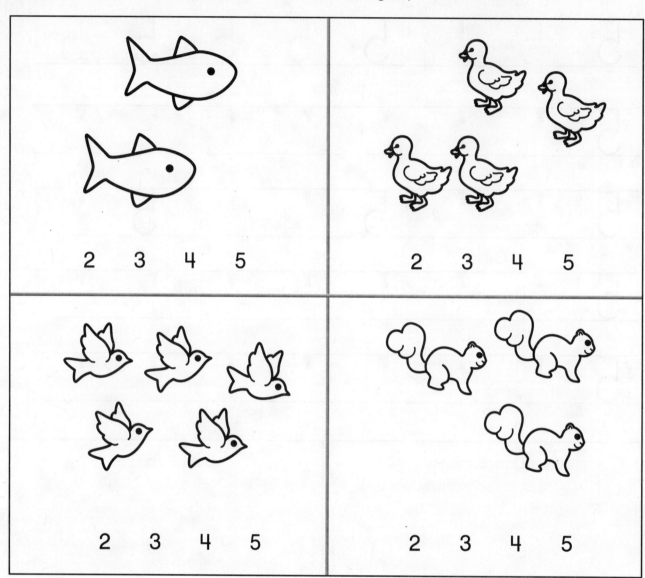

2   3   4   5   2   3   4   5

2   3   4   5   2   3   4   5

Write the number 0.

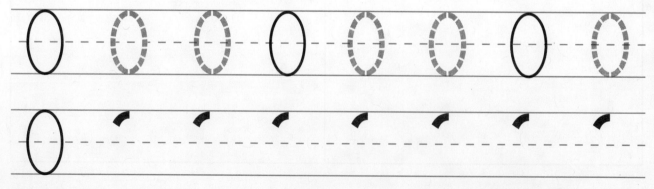

VOCABULARY
order

Connect the dots in **order**.

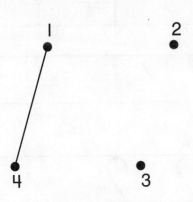

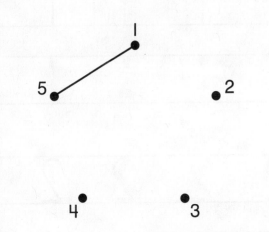

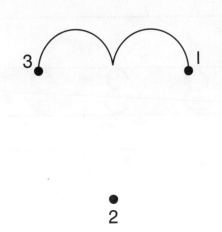

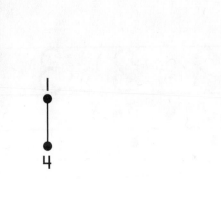

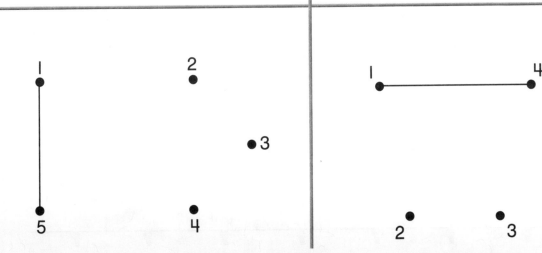

Write the numbers.

1

2 2 2 2 2 2 2 2

2

3 3 3 3 3 3 3 3

3

4 4 4 4 4 4 4 4

4

5 5 5 5 5 5 5 5

5

Color shapes with no straight sides blue.
Color shapes with 4 sides red.

© Houghton Mifflin Harcourt Publishing Company • Image Credits: ©Comstock Images/Getty Images

Draw some shapes with no straight sides.

Draw some shapes with 4 sides.

Focus on Mathematical Practices

Exercises 1–2. Circle the groups of the number. Mark an X on the groups that are not the number.

4

2

Exercises 3–4. Draw.

Draw 3 trees.	Draw 5 flowers.

Name _____

Exercise 5. Draw a line under the circles.

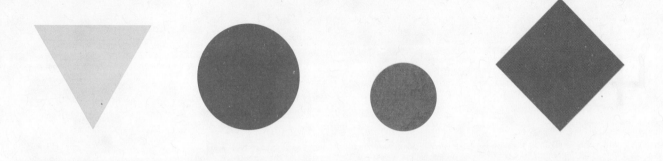

Exercise 6. Draw a line under the rectangles.

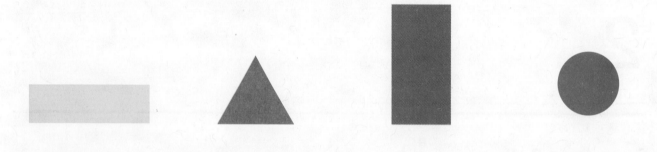

Exercises 7–8. Connect the dots in order.

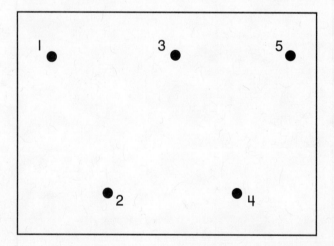 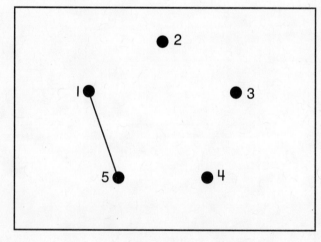

Exercise 9. Write the numbers.

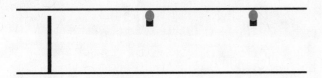

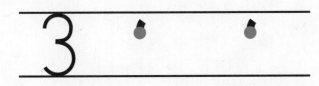

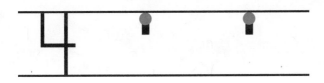

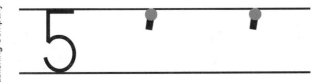

Exercise 10. **Extended Response** Make a drawing. Use 1 circle, 2 triangles, 3 squares, and 4 rectangles.

© Houghton Mifflin Harcourt Publishing Company

Family Letter

Dear Family:

Children are learning to see numbers 6, 7, 8, 9, and 10 as having a 5 and some more. This is called using a 5-group. This visual pattern will help children add, subtract, and understand numbers. It will also help later in multidigit calculation.

Count things at home in 5-groups to help your child see the 5 in 6, 7, 8, 9, and 10. For example, 7 buttons can be counted using 5-groups: "5 and 2 make 7."

Children will see 5-groups in materials they are using in school:

Number Parade

Square-Inch Tiles

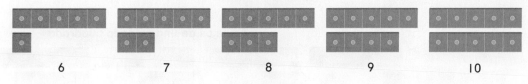

Counters and 5-Counter Strips

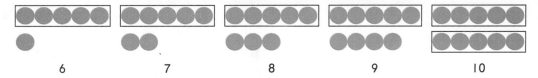

Thank you!

Sincerely,
Your child's teacher

COMMON CORE Unit 2 includes the Common Core Standards for Mathematical Content for Counting and Cardinality K.CC.1, K.CC.2, K.CC.3, K.CC.4, K.CC.4a, K.CC.4b, K.CC.4c, K.CC.5, K.CC.6, K.CC.7; Operations and Algebraic Thinking K.OA.1, K.OA.2, K.OA.3, K.OA.4, K.OA.5; Measurement and Data K.MD.3; Geometry K.G.1, K.G.2, K.G.3, K.G.5 and all Mathematical Practices.

Estimada familia:

Los niños están aprendiendo a ver que los números 6, 7, 8, 9 y 10 contienen el 5 y algo más. Esto se llama usar un grupo de 5. Este patrón visual los ayudará a sumar, a restar y a entender los números. Más adelante también les servirá para los cálculos con números de más de un dígito.

Cuenten cosas en casa haciendo grupos de 5 para que el niño identifique el 5 en el 6, 7, 8 , 9 y 10. Por ejemplo, pueden contar 7 botones haciendo un grupo de 5: "5 más 2 son 7".

Los niños identificarán grupos de 5 en los materiales que usan en la escuela:

Desfile de números

6 7 8 9 10

Azulejos de una pulgada cuadrada

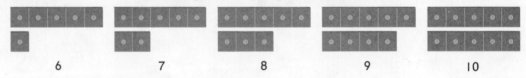

6   7   8   9   10

Fichas y tiras de 5 fichas

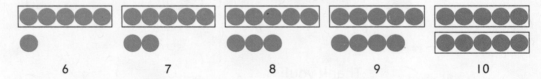

6   7   8   9   10

¡Muchas gracias!

Atentamente,
El maestro de su niño

 COMMON CORE La Unidad 2 incluye los Common Core Standards for Mathematical Content for Counting and Cardinality K.CC.1, K.CC.2, K.CC.3, K.CC.4, K.CC.4a, K.CC.4b, K.CC.4c, K.CC.5, K.CC.6, K.CC.7; Operations and Algebraic Thinking K.OA.1, K.OA.2, K.OA.3, K.OA.4, K.OA.5; Measurement and Data K.MD.3; Geometry K.G.1, K.G.2, K.G.3, K.G.5 and all Mathematical Practices.

Find groups of 1 through 10.

Name _____

Help Puzzled Penguin.

Did Puzzled Penguin write the numbers
1 through 10 in order correctly?

Did I make
a mistake?

| 1 | 2 | 3 | 4 | 6 | 5 | 7 | 8 | 9 | 10 |

Write the numbers 1 through 10 in order.

Write the numbers 0 through 9 in order.

Find Numbers 1–10: Neighborhood Scene

Cut on dashed lines.
Do not cut on solid
lines.

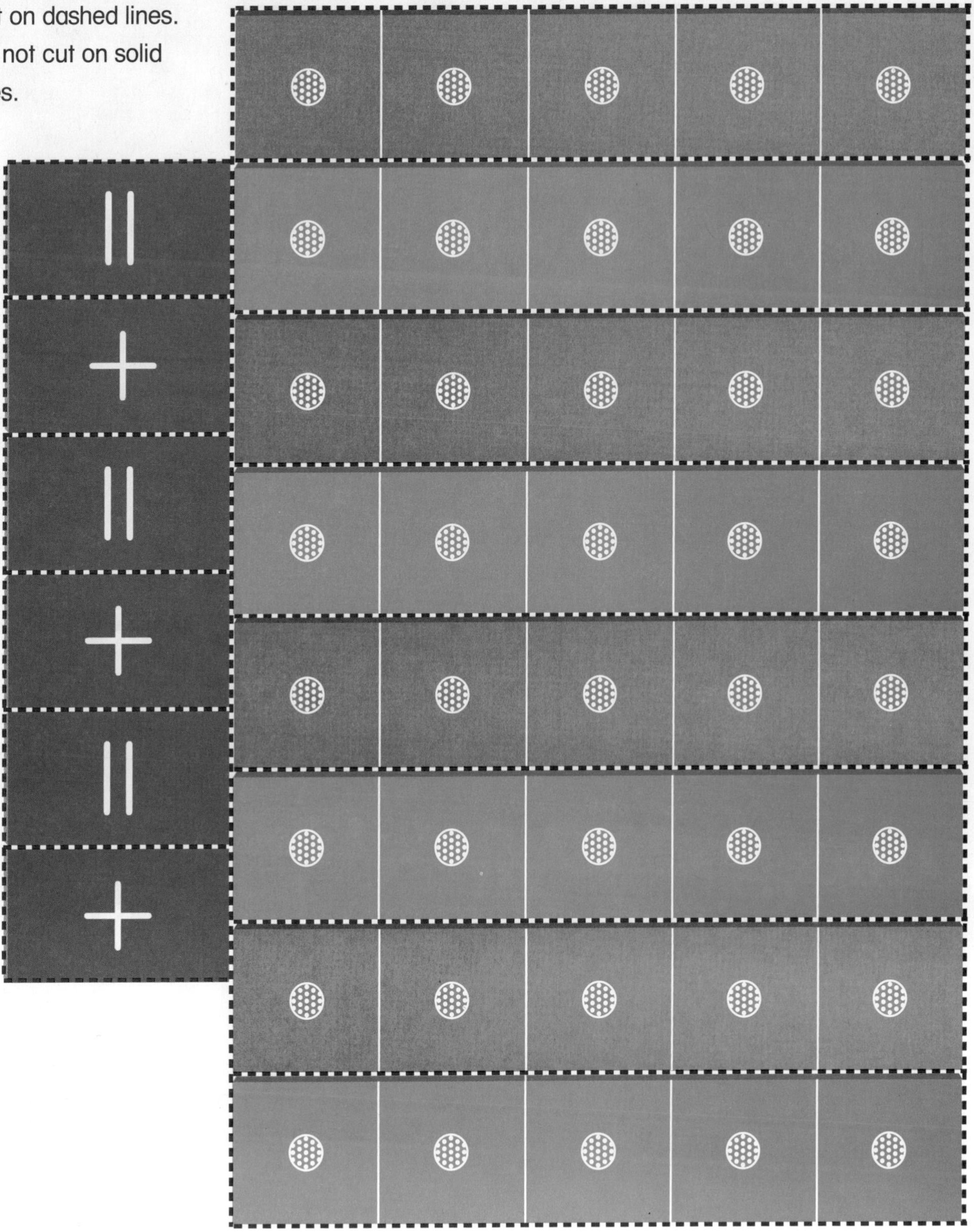

=

+

=

+

=

+

5-Square Tiles **45**

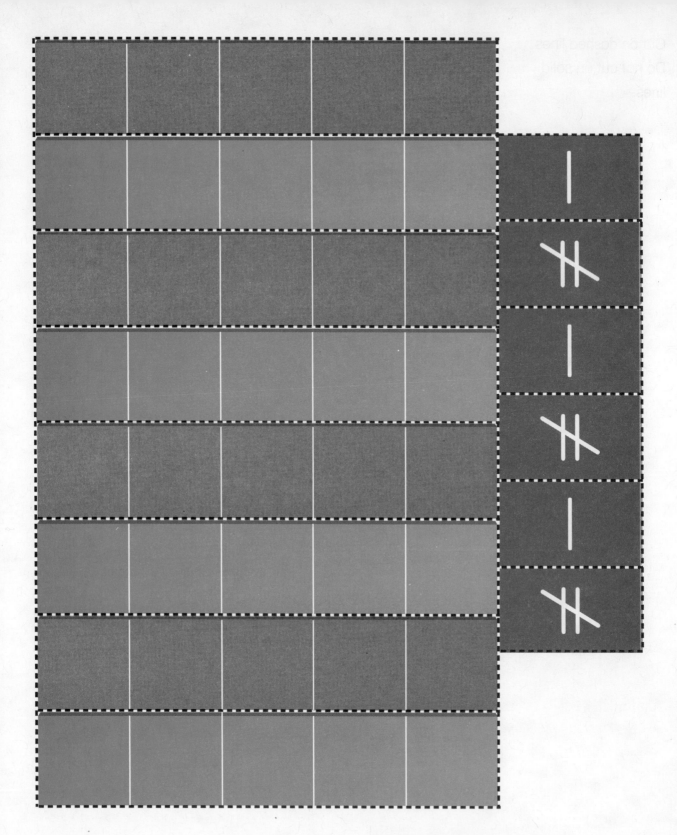

5-Square Tiles

Ring groups of the number. Cross out groups that are not the number.

6

7

8

9

10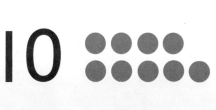

Name

Draw dots to show the number.

6

7

8

9

10

© Houghton Mifflin Harcourt Publishing Company

Family Math Stories

Cut on dashed lines. **Fold** on solid lines and tape at top and bottom.

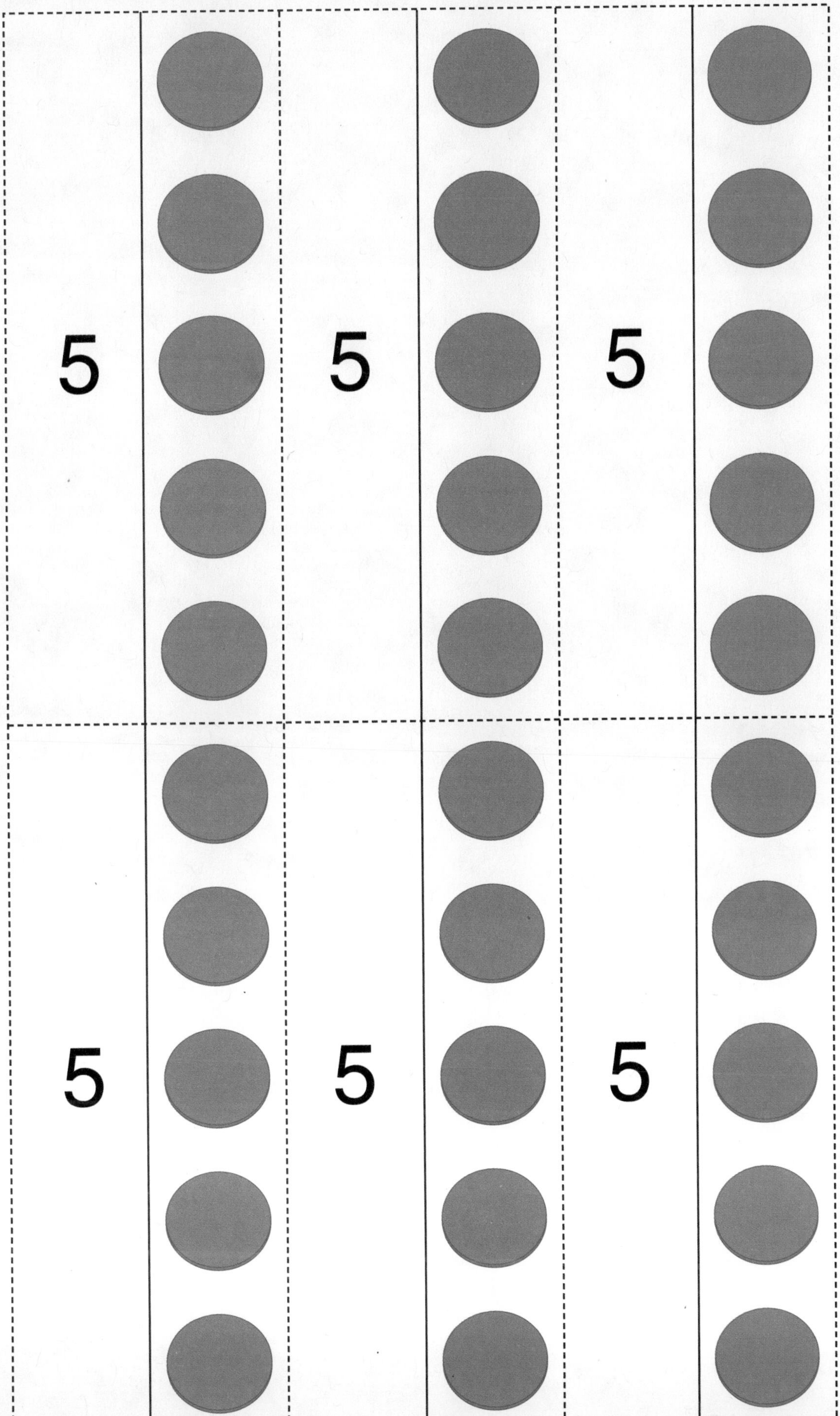

5

5

5

5

5

5

5-Counter Strips

Write the number 6.

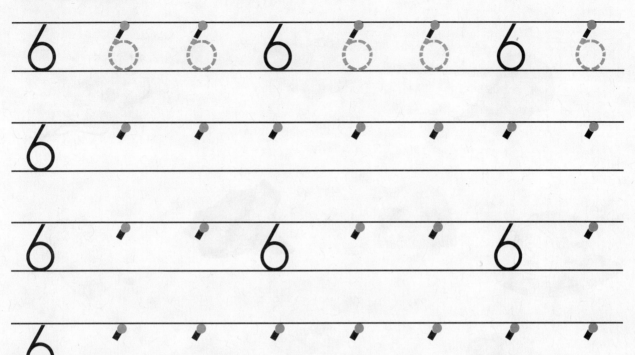

Draw 6 objects.	Draw 6 balls.

Circle 6 hats from the set below.

Write the number 6.

6 6 6 6 6 6 6 6

6 6 6 6 6 6 6 6

6 6 6 6 6 6 6 6

6 6 6 6 6 6 6 6

Tell an addition or subtraction story.

Make a drawing to show how many balloons in all.

VOCABULARY
straight lines

Connect the dots in order. Use parts of **straight lines**.

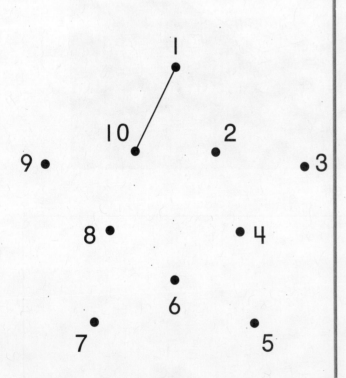

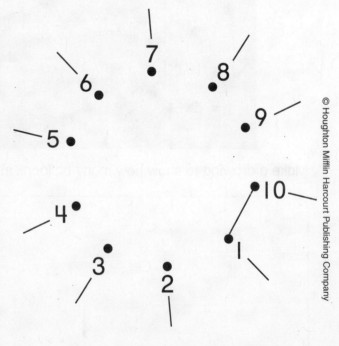

Addition and Subtraction Stories: Playground Scenario

1	2	3	4	5	6
1	**2**	**3**	**4**	**5**	**6**

7	8	9	10
7	**8**	**9**	**1 0**

=	+	=	+	=	+

=	+	=	+	=	+

+/− Tiles, =/≠ Tiles **55**

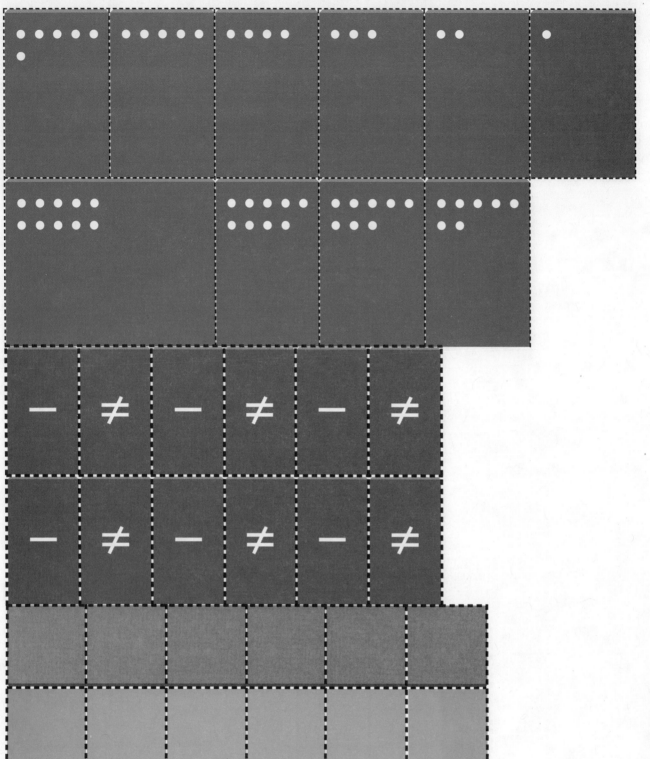

+/− Tiles, =/≠ Tiles

Class Activity

Name _____

Write the numbers 2 and 5.

2 2 2 2 2 2 2 2

2 2 2 2 2 2 2 2

2 2 2 2 2 2 2 2

Draw 2 objects.	Draw 2 circles.

5 5 5 5 5 5 5 5

5 5 5 5 5 5 5 5

5 5 5 5 5 5 5 5

Draw 5 objects.	Draw 5 squares.

2-7 Class Activity

Name ______________________

Write numbers 0 through 5 in order. Use the Number Parade to help.

0 0 0 0 0 0 0 0

0

1 1 1 1 1 1 1 1

1

2 2 2 2 2 2 2 2

2

3 3 3 3 3 3 3 3

3

4 4 4 4 4 4 4 4

4

5 5 5 5 5 5 5 5

5

Write the number 7.

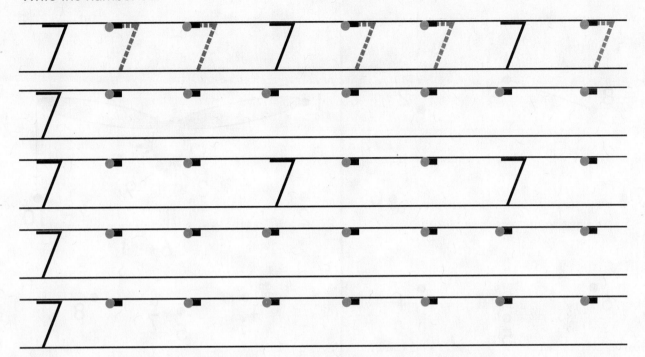

Draw 7 objects.	Draw 7 squares.

Write the numbers 0 through 7 in order.

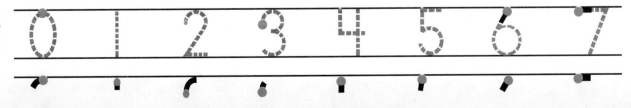

Name _____

Connect the dots in order.

8 • ———• 1

• 2

7 •   • 3

6 •   • 4

    5 •

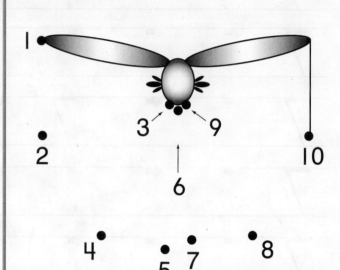

3 •
  • 9

2 •   1 •   • 10

4 •   • 8

5 •   7 • •

3
•

1 •
10 •

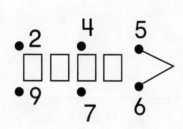

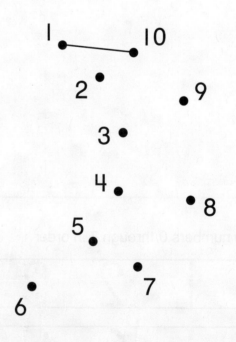

8
•

Name

Use a pencil or marker and trace each number 2 times. Use the color blue to trace the 6s and the color red to trace the 7s.

Write the numbers 1 to 7.

Help Puzzled Penguin.

Did Puzzled Penguin make a mistake?

Look at the numbers below.

Did I make a mistake?

7	6	9	10	8

Write the numbers 6 through 10 in order.

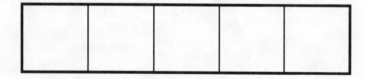

Write the numbers 1 through 10 in order.

Name _____

Write the number 8.

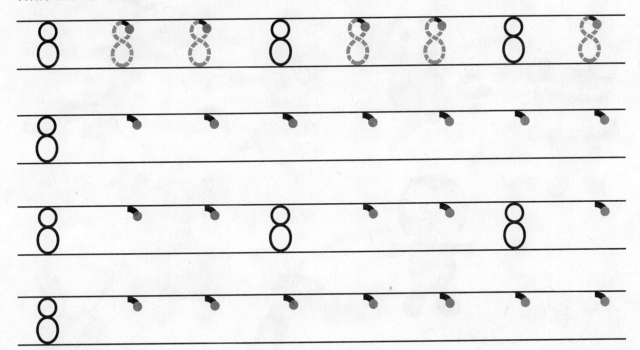

Draw 8 objects.	Draw 8 rectangles.

Circle 8 objects.

Write the number 8.

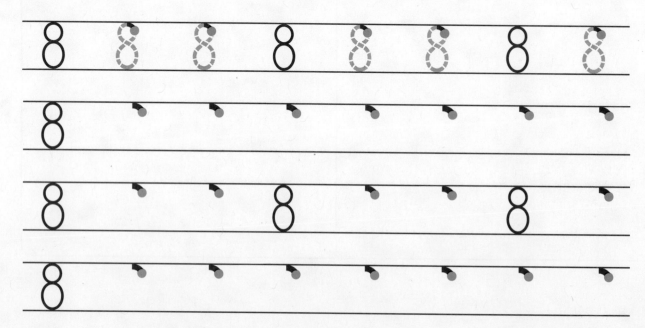

Numbers 6, 7, and 8

Name _____

Tell a math story.

The Neighborhood GARDEN

Addition and Subtraction Stories: Garden Scenario **65**

Write the number 9.

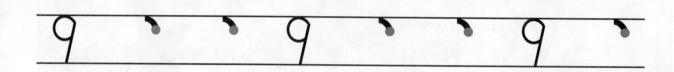

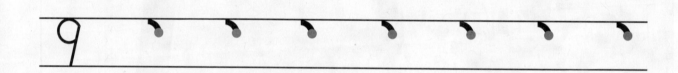

Draw 9 objects.	Draw 9 triangles.

Addition and Subtraction Stories: Garden Scenario

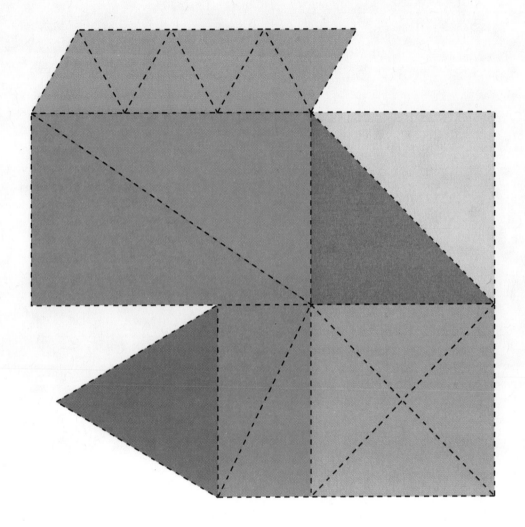

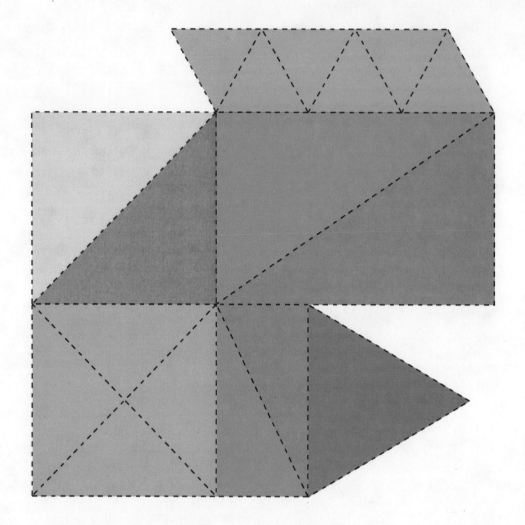

Triangles

Discuss shapes you see.

Trace the shapes.

Draw the same shapes below the pictures.

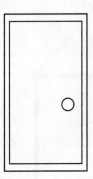

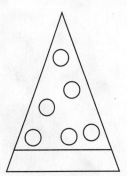

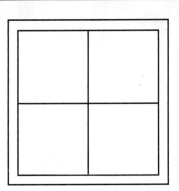

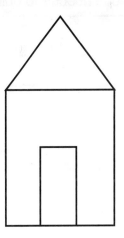

Name shapes you see.

Count the sides of each shape.

Color each shape needed to build the dog house above.

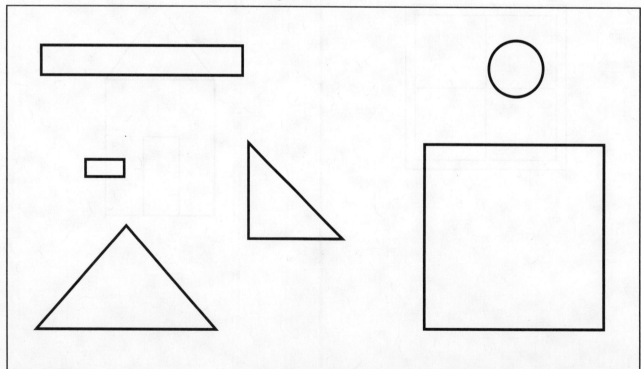

Identify Triangles

Write the number 10.

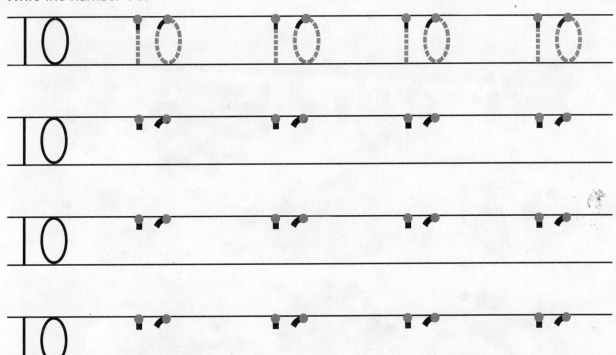

Draw 10 objects.	Draw 10 circles.

Name _____

Circle 10 fish.

Practice writing the number 10.

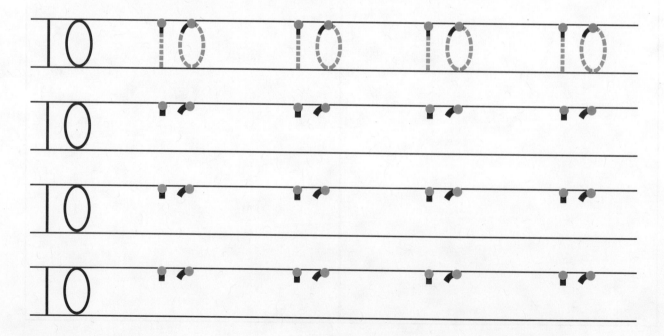

Addition and Subtraction Stories: Family Experiences

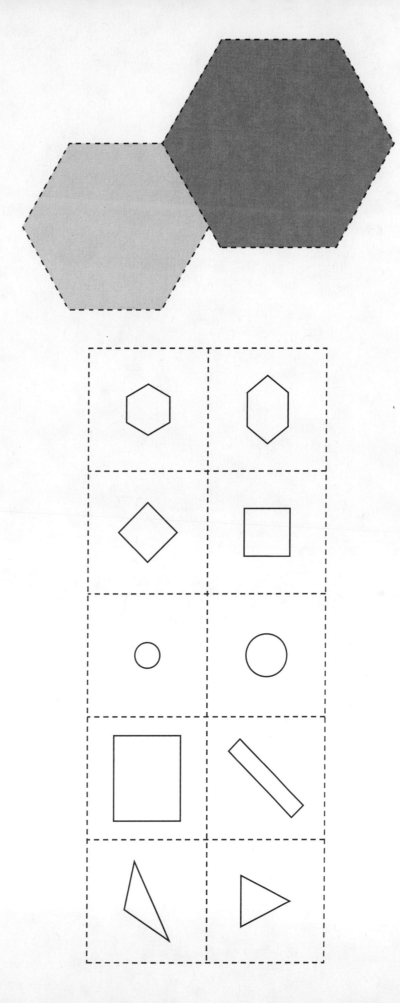

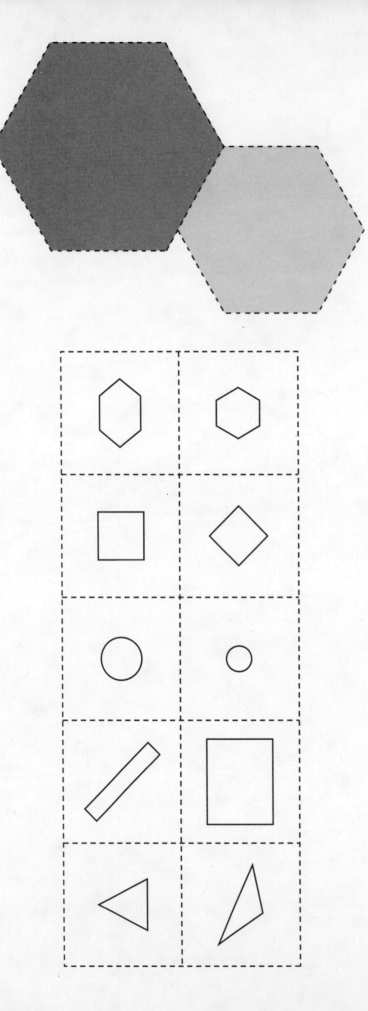

Hexagons

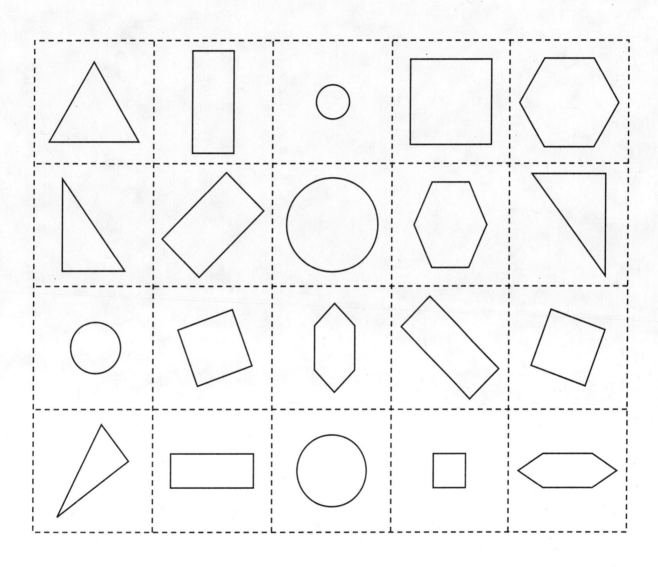

Identify Hexagons **75**

Identify Hexagons

Color the shapes of one kind the same color as below.

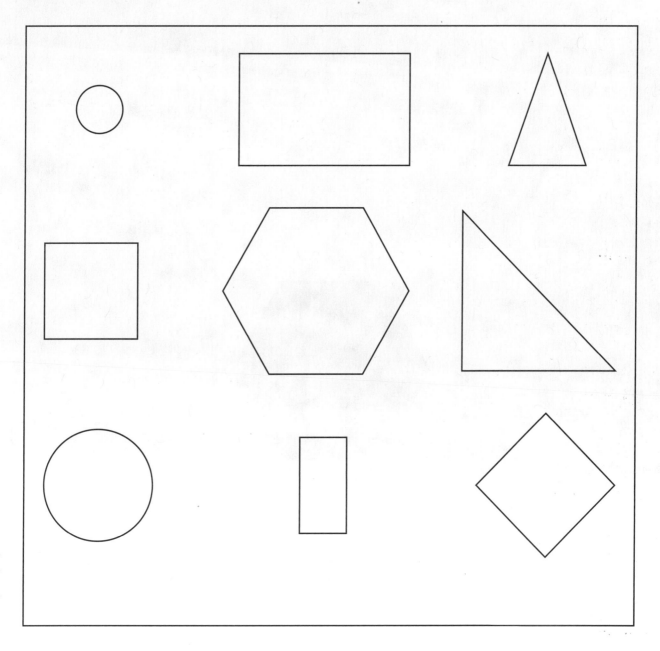

circle   triangle   square   hexagon   rectangle

Use a pencil or marker.

Trace each number two times.

Use the color red to trace the 8s.

Use the color blue to trace the 9s.

Write the numbers 1–10.

Help Puzzled Penguin.

Puzzled Penguin was asked to write the number 6.

Did Puzzled Penguin write the number correctly?

Am I correct?

What number did Puzzled Penguin write?

How can we help Puzzled Penguin write the correct number?

Write the number for Puzzled Penguin.

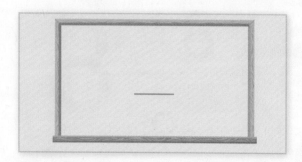

Practice writing the number 6.

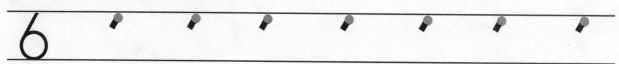

Practice writing the number 9.

Write the numbers 6 through 10 in order.

Number Writing Practice

Name _____

Help Puzzled Penguin.

Did Puzzled Penguin make a mistake?

Look at the numbers below.

Did I make a mistake?

Cross out any numbers that are not in the correct order.

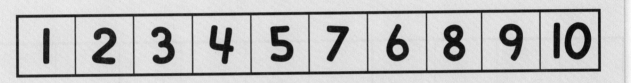

1 2 3 4 5 7 6 8 9 10

Help Puzzled Penguin write the numbers in the correct order.

Cross out any numbers that are not in the correct order.

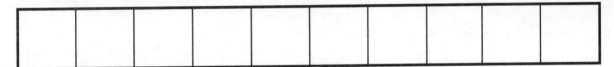

0 1 2 3 4 5 6 7 9 8

Help Puzzled Penguin write the numbers in the correct order.

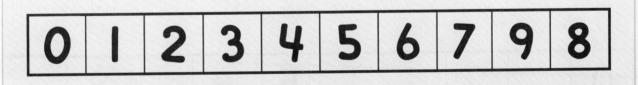

Name _____

Write the numbers 1 through 10 in order.

1	2		4			7			10

	2	3		5	6		8	9	

Write the numbers 0 through 9 in order.

0	1		3	4			7		9

0		2			5	6		8	

More Numbers 1 Through 10: The −1 Pattern

Name _____

Color the shapes of one kind the same color.

Count the number of each shape in the picture.

Write the number.

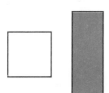

© Houghton Mifflin Harcourt Publishing Company • Image Credits: ©Tony Anderson/Getty Images

Name

Draw a line to match each shape below to a shape in the picture.

circle rectangle triangle square

Focus on Mathematical Practices

Exercises 1-2. Circle groups of the number. Cross Out the groups that are not the number.

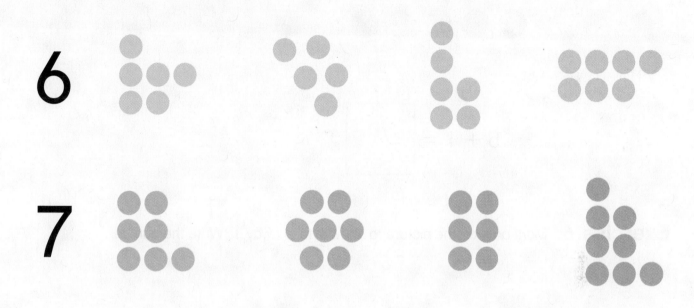

6

7

Exercises 3-4. Connect the dots in order.

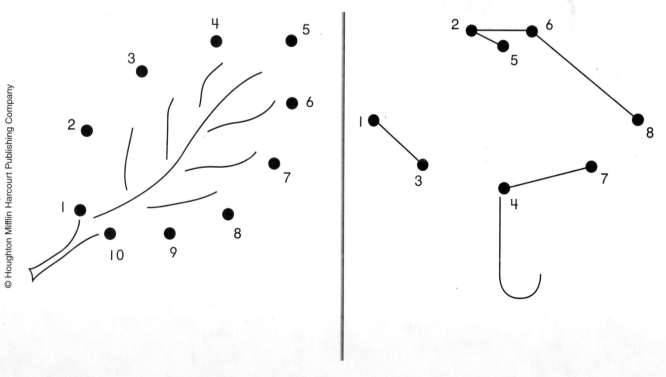

Name _____

Exercise 5. Circle the 5-group. Count the total. Write the number.

$5 + 1 = $ ⬚

Exercise 6. Mark an X on the picture to show 9 take away 1. Write the number.

$9 - 1 = $ ⬚

Name _____

Exercise 7. Draw a line under the triangles.

Exercise 8. Draw a line under the hexagons.

Exercise 9. Write the numbers in order from 5 to 10.

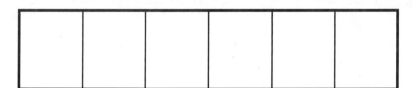

Exercise 10. Extended Response Draw a picture that shows 6 + 1 triangles.
Write how many triangles.

Dear Family:

Your child is starting a new unit on grouping concepts. These concepts provide a foundation for understanding basic math equations. In class, children will learn to find the ten in teen numbers (17 = 10 + 7), break apart numbers to find "partners" (6 = 4 + 2), recognize when numbers are equal or unequal, apply the concepts of *more* and *fewer*, and observe different attributes of shapes.

Being able to group numbers and shapes makes them easier to understand. You can help your child by practicing grouping concepts at home. Here is an example of an activity you can do with your child:

When cleaning up from play, have your child sort the objects before putting them away. Talk about the differences in size, shape, and color, and help your child place the items in groups based on these attributes. For example, the blocks below are sorted by size. They could also be sorted by color.

Thank you for your continued support.

Sincerely,
Your child's teacher

© Houghton Mifflin Harcourt Publishing Company

Estimada familia:

Su niño está empezando una nueva unidad que trata sobre los conceptos de agrupar. Estos conceptos son muy importantes para comprender las ecuaciones matemáticas básicas. Los niños aprenderán a hallar la decena en los números de 11 a 19 ($17 = 10 + 7$), a separar números para hallar "partes" ($6 = 4 + 2$), a reconocer si los números son iguales o no, a aplicar los conceptos de *más* y *menos* y a observar las características de las figuras.

Agrupar números y figuras facilita su comprensión. Usted puede ayudar a su niño practicando en casa los conceptos de agrupar. Aquí tiene un ejemplo de una actividad que pueden hacer:

Cuando estén guardando las cosas después de jugar, pida a su niño que separe los objetos en categorías. Háblele de las diferencias de tamaño, forma y color, y ayúdelo a colocar los objetos en grupos según estas características. Por ejemplo, los bloques que aparecen a continuación están agrupados según su tamaño. También se pueden agrupar según su color.

Gracias por su apoyo.

Atentamente,
El maestro de su niño

 COMMON CORE La Unidad 3 incluye los Common Core Standards for Mathematical Content for Counting and Cardinality K.CC.1, K.CC.2, K.CC.3, K.CC.4, K.CC.4a, K.CC.4b, K.CC.4c, K.CC.5, K.CC.6, K.CC.7; Operations and Algebraic Thinking K.OA.1, K.OA.2, K.OA.3, K.OA.5, ; Number and Operations in Base Ten K.NBT.1; Measurement and Data K.MD.3; Geometry K.G.1, K.G.2, K.G.4 and all Mathematical Practices.

Numbers I–I0 and Math Stories: Park Scene

Color each group of 1 through 10 a different color.

1. Connect the dots in order.

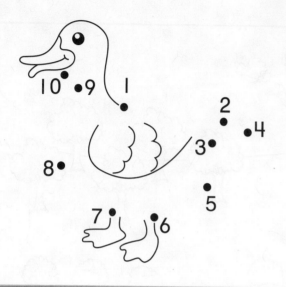

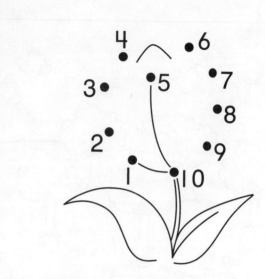

2. Help Puzzled Penguin.

Look at Puzzled Penguin's numbers.

Did Puzzled Penguin write the numbers in order?

Am I correct?

1	2	4	3	5	6	7	8	9	10

Write the numbers 1 through 10 in order.

Numbers 1–10 and Math Stories: Park Scene

Cut on dashed lines. **Fold** on solid lines and tape at top and bottom.

10

10

10

10-Counter Strips **93**

Name _____

Connect the dots from 1 through 20 and color the Ten Bug.

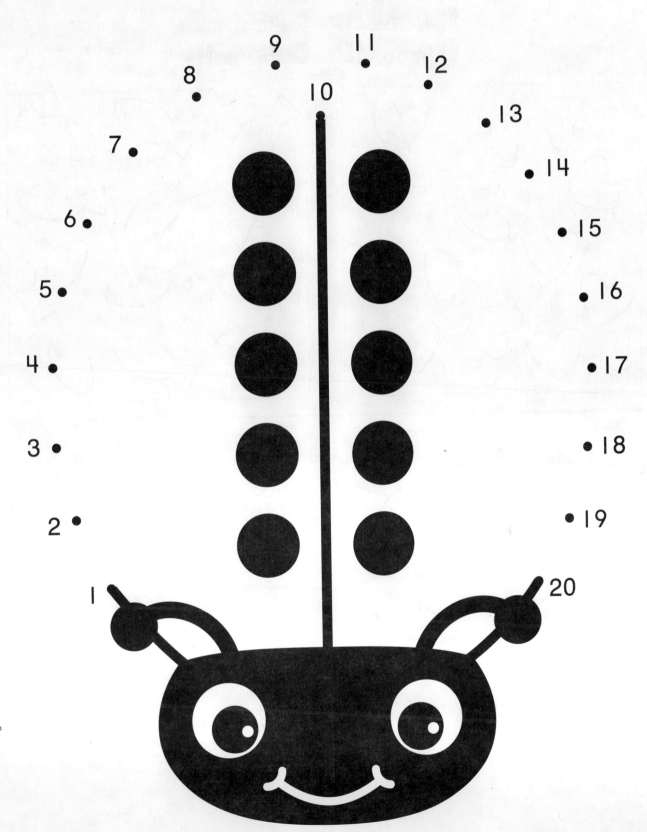

Name _____

Circle a group of 10 in each box. Count and color the items. Use the colors shown.

11—red   13—yellow

12—blue   14—green

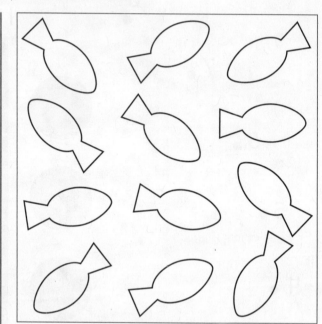

Dear Family:

Your child is learning about partners of numbers. We call the number pairs that make up a number "partners" because they go together to make that number. For example,

6 has partners: 1 and 5   2 and 4   3 and 3

$6 = 1 + 5$

$6 = 2 + 4$

$6 = 3 + 3$

The partner idea is very important for understanding numbers. It will help your child understand addition and subtraction. You can help your child see partners in everyday life. When you have a small number of objects, for example, 5 crackers, you can ask your child to make the partners of 5. Your child can show 1 and 4 crackers and can also show 2 and 3 crackers. Doing this often with different objects will help your child understand numbers.

Thank you!

Sincerely,
Your child's teacher

COMMON CORE

Unit 3 includes the Common Core Standards for Mathematical Content for Counting and Cardinality K.CC.1, K.CC.2, K.CC.3, K.CC.4, K.CC.4a, K.CC.4b, K.CC.4c, K.CC.5, K.CC.6, K.CC.7; Operations and Algebraic Thinking K.OA.1, K.OA.2, K.OA.3, K.OA.5, ; Number and Operations in Base Ten K.NBT.1; Measurement and Data K.MD.3; Geometry K.G.1, K.G.2, K.G.4 and all Mathematical Practices.

Estimada familia:

Su niño está aprendiendo sobre las partes de los números. Llamamos "partes" a los pares de números que pueden juntarse para formar un determinado número. Por ejemplo,

6 tiene las partes: 1 y 5   2 y 4   3 y 3

$6 = 1 + 5$

$6 = 2 + 4$

$6 = 3 + 3$

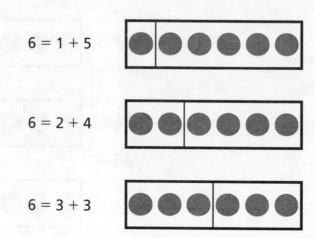

La idea de las partes es muy importante para entender los números. Ayudará a su niño a entender la suma y la resta. Ud. puede ayudar a su niño a ver partes en la vida diaria. Cuando tenga un pequeño número de objetos, por ejemplo 5 galletas, puede pedirle a su niño que muestre las partes de 5. Su niño puede mostrar 1 galleta y 4 galletas y también 2 galletas y 3 galletas. Hacer esto a menudo con distintos objetos puede ayudar a su niño a entender los números.

¡Gracias!

Atentamente,
El maestro de su niño

COMMON CORE

La Unidad 3 incluye los Common Core Standards for Mathematical Content for Counting and Cardinality K.CC.1, K.CC.2, K.CC.3, K.CC.4, K.CC.4a, K.CC.4b, K.CC.4c, K.CC.5, K.CC.6, K.CC.7; Operations and Algebraic Thinking K.OA.1, K.OA.2, K.OA.3, K.OA.5; Number and Operations in Base Ten K.NBT.1; Measurement and Data K.MD.3; Geometry K.G.1, K.G.2, K.G.4 and all Mathematical Practices.

Name _____

Write the number.

1.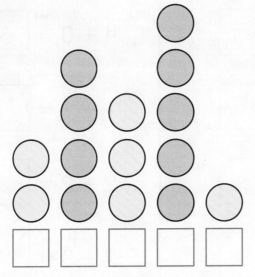

2.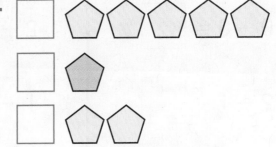

3.

4.

5. Write the numbers 1–10.

Name _____

PATH to
FLUENCY

6. Add the numbers.

0 + 3 = ☐   2 + 0 = ☐   4 + 0 = ☐

2 + 1 = ☐   1 + 4 = ☐   1 + 1 = ☐

0 + 2 = ☐   1 + 2 = ☐   2 + 2 = ☐

0 + 3 = ☐   3 + 1 = ☐   2 + 3 = ☐

4 + 1 = ☐   5 + 0 = ☐   1 + 4 = ☐

7. Subtract the numbers.

3 − 0 = ☐   2 − 0 = ☐   4 − 0 = ☐

4 − 1 = ☐   5 − 1 = ☐   1 − 1 = ☐

5 − 2 = ☐   4 − 2 = ☐   3 − 2 = ☐

3 − 3 = ☐   5 − 3 = ☐   4 − 3 = ☐

5 − 4 = ☐   4 − 4 = ☐   5 − 5 = ☐

Addition and Subtraction Stories: Park Scene

Dear Family:

When children first start counting, they count objects one at a time. Helping children see 5-groups and 10-groups enables them to understand larger (greater) numbers. We are learning that if we can see groups of objects as 5-groups and 10-groups, then we can understand greater numbers. Children learn to make these groups with objects. Later, they will see them as organized groups in their minds.

Your child is learning that the teen numbers 11, 12, 13, 14, 15, 16, 17, 18, and 19 each have a 10 inside: 11 = 10 + 1, 12 = 10 + 2, and so on through 19 = 10 + 9.

Have your child practice counting groups of objects. Your child can find and separate the 10-group from the total quantity to see the 10 hiding inside the teen number.

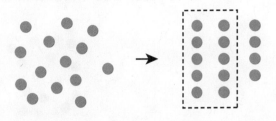

fourteen   is   ten and four

Your child can then show this number by using the number cards on the next page.

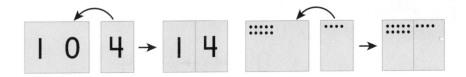

Thank you for your cooperation!

Sincerely,
Your child's teacher

Estimada familia:

Cuando los niños empiezan a contar, suelen contar los objetos uno por uno. Ayudarlos a ver los objetos en grupos de 5 y grupos de 10, les facilita el aprendizaje de números más grandes (mayores). Estamos aprendiendo que si podemos ver grupos de objetos como grupos de 5 y grupos de 10, entonces podemos entender números más grandes. Los niños aprenden a formar estos grupos con objetos. Más adelante, los verán mentalmente como grupos organizados.

Su niño está aprendiendo que los números 11, 12, 13, 14, 15, 16, 17, 18 y 19 contienen 10: $11 = 10 + 1$, $12 = 10 + 2$, y así sucesivamente, hasta $19 = 10 + 9$.

Pida a su niño que practique contando grupos de objetos. Su niño puede separar el grupo de 10 de la cantidad total, para ver el 10 escondido en los números de 11 a 19.

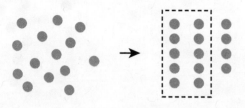

catorce   es   diez más cuatro

Después, su niño puede mostrar este número usando las tarjetas de números de la página siguiente.

¡Gracias por su colaboración!

Atentamente,
El maestro de su niño

 COMMON CORE

La Unidad 3 incluye los Common Core Standards for Mathematical Content for Counting and Cardinality K.CC.1, K.CC.2, K.CC.3, K.CC.4, K.CC.4a, K.CC.4b, K.CC.4c, K.CC.5, K.CC.6, K.CC.7; Operations and Algebraic Thinking K.OA.1, K.OA.2, K.OA.3, K.OA.5; Number and Operations in Base Ten K.NBT.1; Measurement and Data K.MD.3; Geometry K.G.1, K.G.2, K.G.4 and all Mathematical Practices.

At Home Number Cards

Tarjetas de números para practicar en casa

1	2	3	4	5
6	7	8	9	10

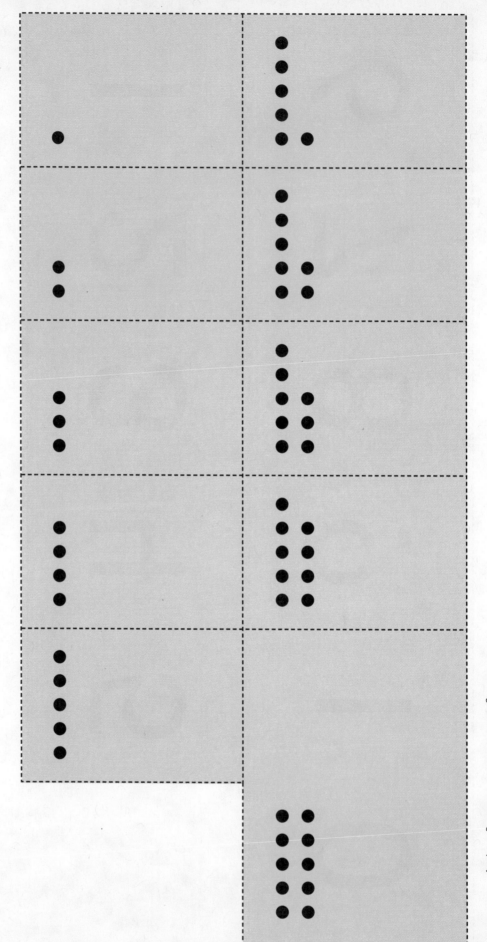

3-5
Class Activity

Name ______________________

VOCABULARY
5-group

1. Draw the circles on the Number Parade. Use a **5-group**.

6	7	8	9	10

2. Use the 5-group. Draw to show the number.

9 = ○○○○○

6 = ○○○○○

8 = ○○○○○

10 = ○○○○○

7 = ○○○○○

3. Write the number.

☐ = ○○○○○ ○○○○ ☐ = ○○○○○ ○○○○

☐ = ○○○○○ ☐ = ○○○○○ ○○○

☐ = ○○○○ ☐ = ○○○○○ ○○

☐ = ○○○○○ ○ ☐ = ○○○○○ ○

☐ = ○○ ☐ = ○○○○○ ○○

☐ = ○○○○○ ○○○ ☐ = ○○○

4. Write the number 11.

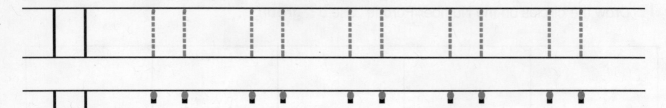

5. Write the number 12.

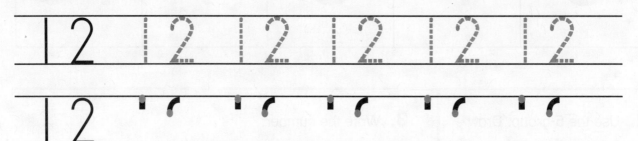

6. Add the numbers.

PATH to
FLUENCY

$2 + 0 = \boxed{}$ $0 + 3 = \boxed{}$ $5 + 0 = \boxed{}$

$1 + 1 = \boxed{}$ $1 + 2 = \boxed{}$ $4 + 1 = \boxed{}$

$2 + 2 = \boxed{}$ $3 + 2 = \boxed{}$ $2 + 3 = \boxed{}$

7. Subtract the numbers.

$4 - 0 = \boxed{}$ $1 - 0 = \boxed{}$ $5 - 0 = \boxed{}$

$4 - 1 = \boxed{}$ $2 - 1 = \boxed{}$ $3 - 1 = \boxed{}$

$4 - 2 = \boxed{}$ $5 - 2 = \boxed{}$ $5 - 3 = \boxed{}$

More Groups of 10

Dear Family:

When children first learn to write numbers, emphasis is placed on forming the numbers correctly. Children begin by tracing, and then are provided with starting points for their pencils. Learning the correct technique helps children learn to write numbers neatly and consistently.

After awhile, children no longer need these hints and are able to write without guide lines or starting points. It is easier for many children to write smaller figures, since they have greater control of the writing tool. With practice, children will gain confidence and speed in writing numbers.

In Unit 3, children continue to practice writing numbers, including 2-digit numbers from 11 to 20. They are already familiar with the individual numbers they will be using. When writing 2-digit numbers, children learn the proper placement and spacing between numbers. The numbers should not be too close together or too far apart, but just the right distance to be read and understood.

Please help and encourage your child as he or she learns to write numbers. This will take time and practice.

Thank you!

Sincerely,
Your child's teacher

COMMON CORE Unit 3 includes the Common Core Standards for Mathematical Content for Counting and Cardinality K.CC.1, K.CC.2, K.CC.3, K.CC.4, K.CC.4a, K.CC.4b, K.CC.4c, K.CC.5, K.CC.6, K.CC.7; Operations and Algebraic Thinking K.OA.1, K.OA.2, K.OA.3, K.OA.5, ; Number and Operations in Base Ten K.NBT.1; Measurement and Data K.MD.3; Geometry K.G.1, K.G.2, K.G.4 and all Mathematical Practices.

Estimada familia:

Cuando los niños aprenden a escribir los números, se enfatiza que deben trazarlos correctamente. Se comienza calcando y luego, se les proporcionan puntos desde donde deben comenzar con sus lápices. Aprender la técnica exacta les servirá a los niños para escribir consistentemente los números de manera correcta.

Después de un tiempo, ya no necesitan estas pistas y pueden escribir sin líneas que les guíen y sin puntos donde comenzar. Es más fácil para muchos niños trazar números pequeños, ya que así tienen más control del instrumento de escritura. Con práctica, los niños adquirirán confianza y velocidad para escribir los números.

En la Unidad 3, los niños continúan practicando la escritura de números, incluyendo los números de 2 dígitos del 11 al 20. Ya están familiarizados con los números individuales que estarán usando. Al escribir números de 2 dígitos, deben aprender su colocación correcta y la distancia correcta que debe haber entre los dígitos. No deben estar demasiado juntos ni demasiado separados, la distancia debe ser adecuada para poder leerlos y comprenderlos.

Por favor ayude a su niño a escribir los números. Esto requerirá tiempo y práctica. Anímelo y apóyelo durante el aprendizaje.

¡Gracias!

Atentamente,
El maestro de su niño

COMMON CORE

La Unidad 3 incluye los Common Core Standards for Mathematical Content for Counting and Cardinality K.CC.1, K.CC.2, K.CC.3, K.CC.4, K.CC.4a, K.CC.4b, K.CC.4c, K.CC.5, K.CC.6, K.CC.7; Operations and Algebraic Thinking K.OA.1, K.OA.2, K.OA.3, K.OA.5; Number and Operations in Base Ten K.NBT.1; Measurement and Data K.MD.3; Geometry K.G.1, K.G.2, K.G.4 and all Mathematical Practices.

1. Write the number 13.

$$3 \quad 3 \quad 3 \quad 3 \quad 3 \quad 3$$

$$3$$

$$3$$

$$3$$

2. Write the number 14.

$$14 \quad 14 \quad 14 \quad 14 \quad 14$$

$$14$$

$$14$$

$$14$$

3. Add the numbers.

0 + 2 = ☐	1 + 0 = ☐	0 + 5 = ☐
3 + 1 = ☐	1 + 3 = ☐	0 + 1 = ☐
2 + 2 = ☐	2 + 1 = ☐	2 + 3 = ☐
2 + 3 = ☐	3 + 1 = ☐	3 + 0 = ☐
0 + 4 = ☐	4 + 1 = ☐	5 + 0 = ☐

4. Subtract the numbers.

1 − 0 = ☐	4 − 0 = ☐	2 − 0 = ☐
5 − 1 = ☐	3 − 1 = ☐	4 − 1 = ☐
3 − 2 = ☐	2 − 2 = ☐	4 − 2 = ☐
5 − 3 = ☐	4 − 3 = ☐	3 − 3 = ☐
4 − 4 = ☐	5 − 5 = ☐	5 − 4 = ☐

Model Partners Through 6 with Counters

1. Draw the circles on the Number Parade. Use a **5-group**.

6	7	8	9	10

2. Use the 5-group. Draw to show the number.

6 = ⬜ (○○○○○)

7 = ⬜ (○○○○○)

8 = ⬜ (○○○)

9 = ⬜ (○○○○○)

10 = ⬜ (○○○○○)

3. Write the number.

⬜ = (○○○)   ⬜ = (○○○○○ / ○○)

⬜ = (○○○○○ / ○○○)   ⬜ = (○○○○○ / ○)

⬜ = (○○)   ⬜ = (○○○○○ / ○○)

⬜ = (○○○○○ / ○○○)   ⬜ = (○○○○)

⬜ = (○○○○○ / ○)   ⬜ = (○○○○○ / ○○○○)

⬜ = (○○○○○ / ○○○○○)   ⬜ = (○○○○○)

4. Write the number 15.

15 15 15 15 15 15

15

5. Write the number 16.

16 16 16 16 16 16

16

6. Add the numbers.

PATH to FLUENCY

$5 + 0 = \square$	$0 + 3 = \square$	$4 + 0 = \square$
$2 + 1 = \square$	$1 + 2 = \square$	$1 + 1 = \square$
$2 + 2 = \square$	$3 + 2 = \square$	$1 + 4 = \square$

7. Subtract the numbers.

$3 - 0 = \square$	$1 - 0 = \square$	$2 - 0 = \square$
$2 - 1 = \square$	$5 - 1 = \square$	$3 - 1 = \square$
$5 - 2 = \square$	$5 - 4 = \square$	$4 - 2 = \square$

More Addition and Subtraction Stories: Park Scene

Build the shape.

1.

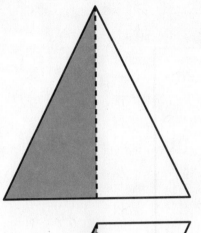

2.

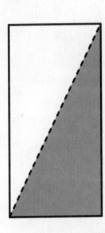

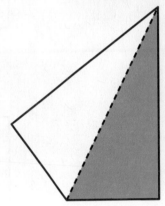

3.

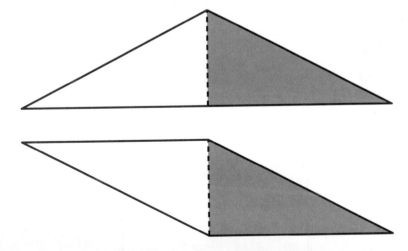

Build. Trace the shapes. Color.

4. Use 4 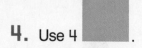.

5. Use 4 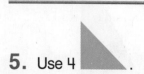.

6. Use 1 ▮ and 1 ▮.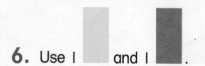

Make New Shapes

Name _____

Build. Trace the shapes. Color.

1.

2.

3.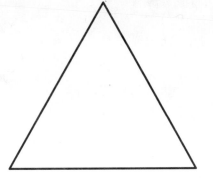

4.

Name _____

Build. Trace the shapes. Color.

5.

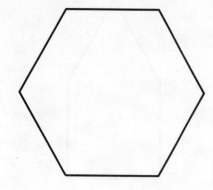

6.

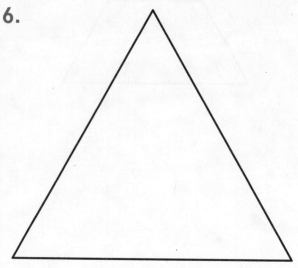

Build a shape. Trace the outline of the shape.

7.

Make New Shapes

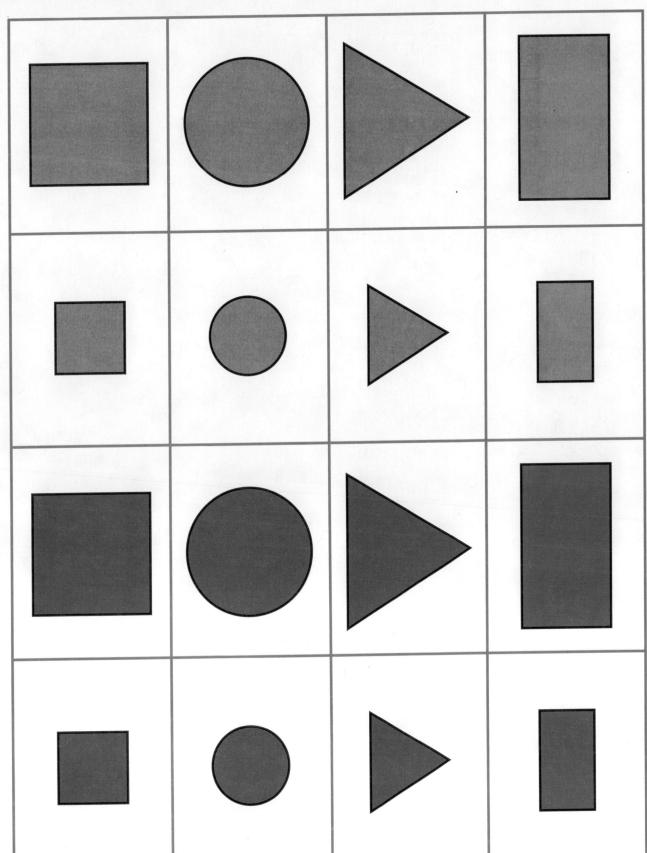

Sorting Cards **117**

Sorting Cards

Sorting Cards

VOCABULARY
5-groups

1. Draw circles for 1–10.
   Show the **5-groups**.

1	
2	
3	
4	
5	
6	
7	
8	○○○○○ ○○○
9	
10	

2. Use the 5-group. Draw to show the number.

9 = ○○○○○

7 = ○○○○○

8 = ○○○○○

10 = ○○○○○

6 = ○○○○○

9 = ○○○○○

7 = ○○○○○

8 = ○○○○○

3. Write the number.

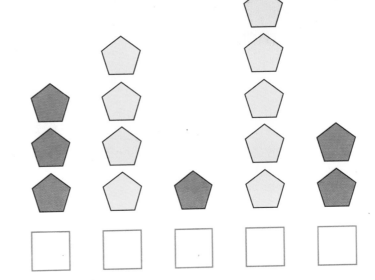

Name _____

Help Puzzled Penguin.

4. Look at Puzzled Penguin's answers.

○○○○
○   = 6

○○○○○
○○○   = 9

○○○○○
○○   = 7

○○○○○
○○○○   = 8

Am I correct?

5. Look at what Puzzled Penguin wrote.

8 fingers

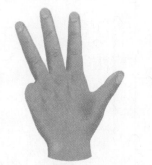

Show 4 + 2 on your fingers another way.

_____ fingers

Practice Addition and Subtraction Stories: Park Scene

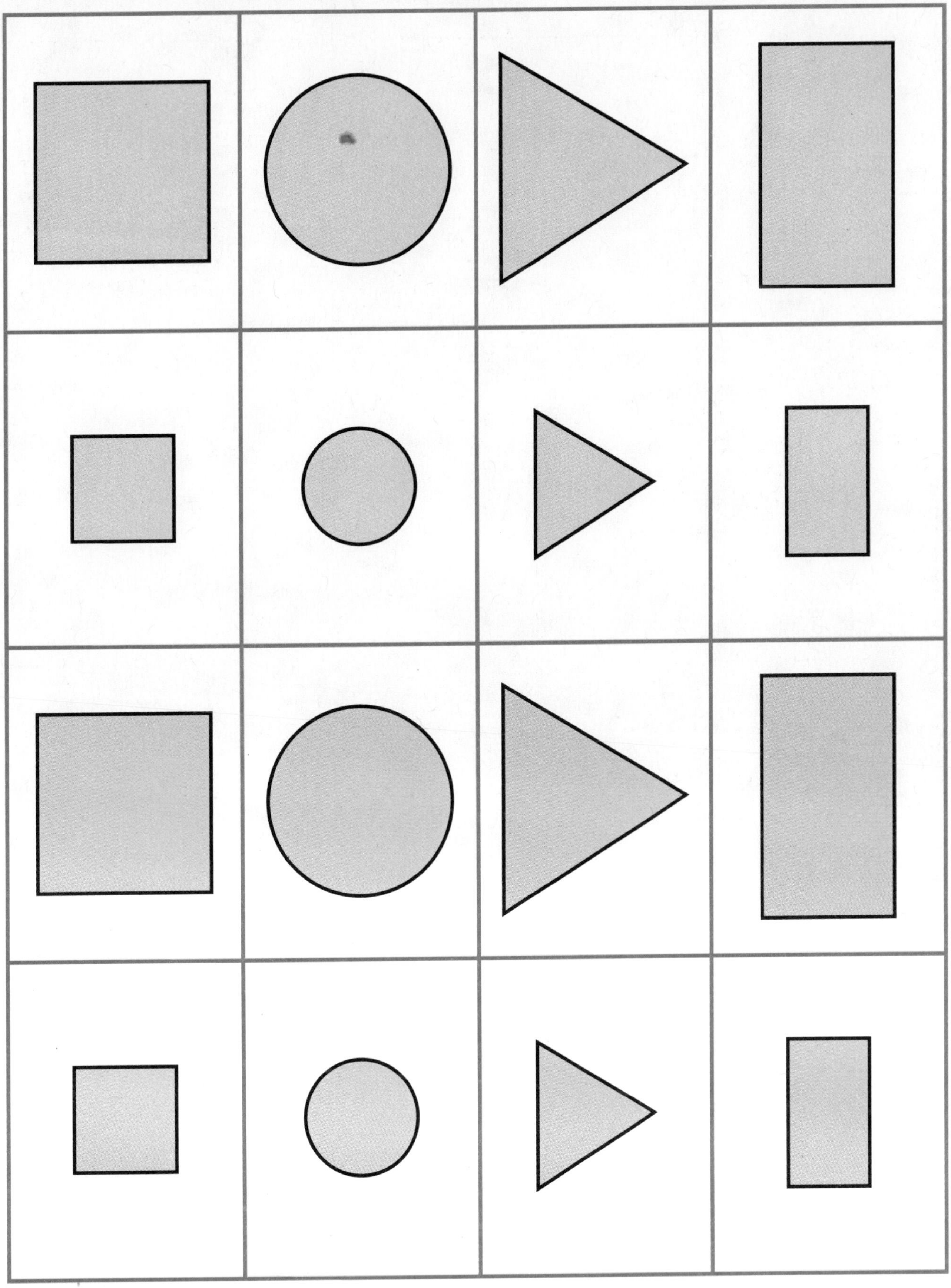

Sorting Cards

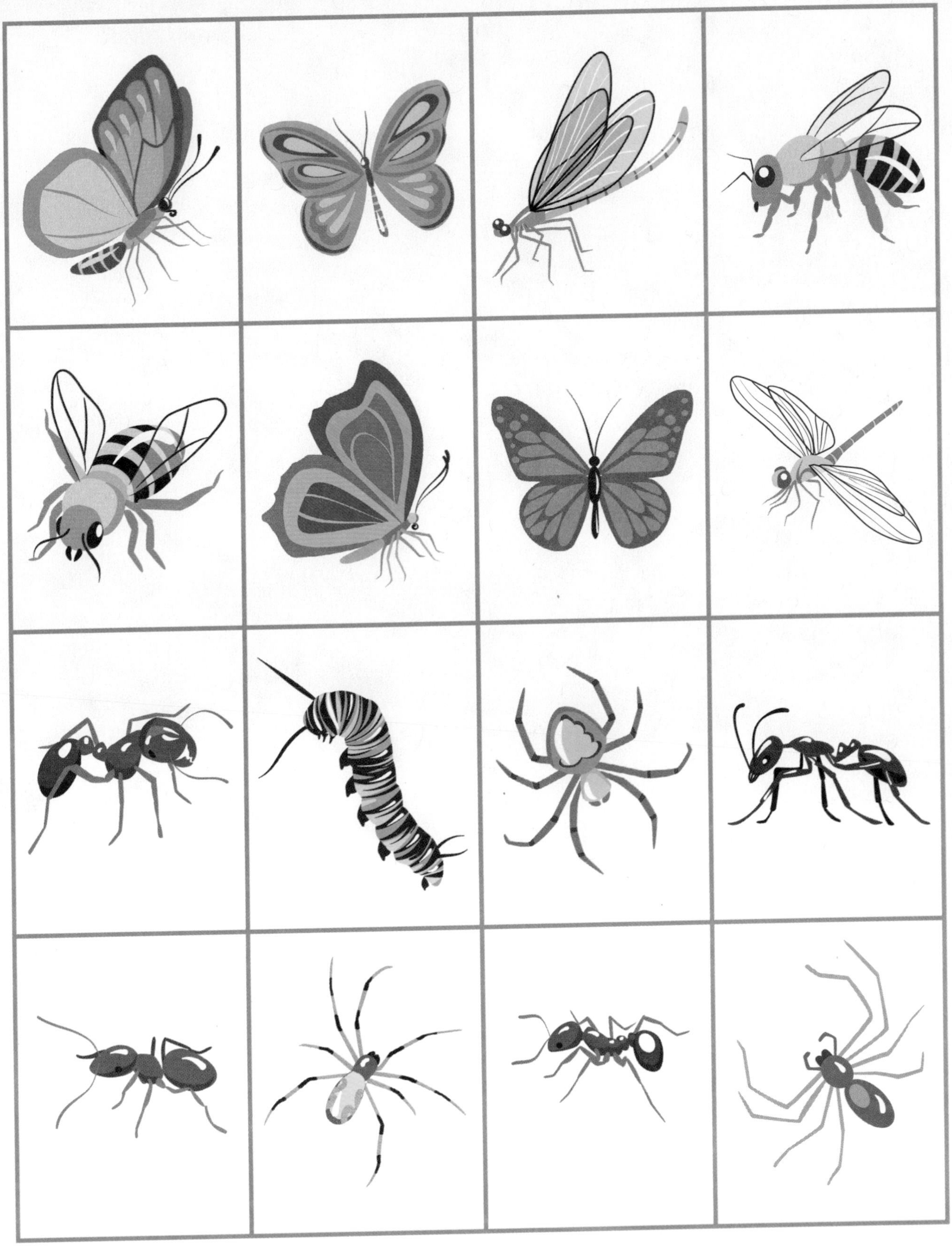

Sorting Cards

VOCABULARY
equal sign (=)
is not equal to sign (≠)

1. Draw circles for 1–10. Show the 5-group.

1	2	3	4	5	6	7	8	9	10
								○○○○○○○○○	

2. Write each number and an **equal sign (=)** or an **is not equal to sign (≠)**.

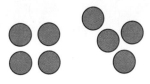

$$2 \neq 4$$

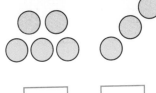

⬜ ⬜

⬜ ⬜

⬜ ⬜

⬜ ⬜

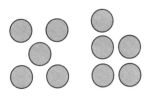

⬜ ⬜

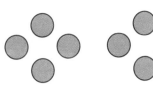

⬜ ⬜

⬜ ⬜

PATH to FLUENCY

3. Add the numbers.

$0 + 4 =$ ☐

$3 + 1 =$ ☐

$2 + 2 =$ ☐

$2 + 3 =$ ☐

$4 + 0 =$ ☐

$0 + 0 =$ ☐

$1 + 2 =$ ☐

$2 + 0 =$ ☐

$3 + 1 =$ ☐

$1 + 4 =$ ☐

$1 + 0 =$ ☐

$4 + 1 =$ ☐

$0 + 2 =$ ☐

$3 + 2 =$ ☐

$0 + 5 =$ ☐

4. Subtract the numbers.

$0 - 0 =$ ☐

$3 - 1 =$ ☐

$5 - 2 =$ ☐

$4 - 3 =$ ☐

$4 - 4 =$ ☐

$1 - 0 =$ ☐

$4 - 1 =$ ☐

$3 - 2 =$ ☐

$5 - 3 =$ ☐

$5 - 2 =$ ☐

$4 - 0 =$ ☐

$2 - 1 =$ ☐

$2 - 2 =$ ☐

$3 - 3 =$ ☐

$5 - 1 =$ ☐

Practice Classifying

Name _____

1. Write the number. Draw it using the 5-group.

  = ☐

○○○○○

 = ☐

○○○○○

 = ☐

○○○○○

 = ☐

○○○○○

2. Use the 5-group. Draw to show the number.

7 = ◯◯◯◯◯

10 = ◯◯◯◯◯

9 = ◯◯◯◯◯

7 = ◯◯◯◯◯

6 = ◯◯◯◯◯

6 = ◯◯◯◯◯

8 = ◯◯◯◯◯

9 = ◯◯◯◯◯

3. Write the number.

◯◯◯◯◯ ◯ = ☐

◯◯◯◯◯ ◯◯ = ☐

◯◯◯◯◯ ◯◯ = ☐

◯◯◯◯◯ ◯◯◯ = ☐

◯◯◯◯ = ☐

◯◯◯◯ = ☐

◯◯◯◯◯ ◯◯◯ = ☐

◯◯◯◯◯ ◯◯◯◯ = ☐

4. Draw a ring around every 5-group.

Write the numbers shown by the circles.

5. Look at what Puzzled Penguin drew.

Help Puzzled Penguin.

1	2	3	4	5	6	7	8	9	10

Am I correct?

Build Teen Numbers

1. Draw circles for 1–10. Show the 5-group.

1	2	3	4	5	6	7	8	9	10
							○○○○○ ○○○		

2. Write each number and an **equal sign (=)** or an **is not equal to sign (≠)**.

$\boxed{5} = \boxed{5}$

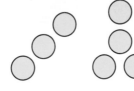

$\square \quad \square$

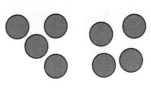

$\square \quad \square$

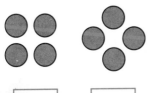

$\square \quad \square$

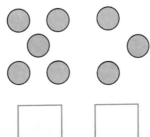

$\square \quad \square$

$\square \quad \square$

3. Write the number 15.

15 15 15 15 15 15

15

4. Write the number 16.

16 16 16 16 16 16

16

PATH to
FLUENCY

5. Add the numbers.

0 + 2 = ☐	0 + 0 = ☐	3 + 0 = ☐
1 + 3 = ☐	1 + 2 = ☐	4 + 1 = ☐
2 + 3 = ☐	3 + 2 = ☐	0 + 4 = ☐

6. Subtract the numbers.

4 − 0 = ☐	0 − 0 = ☐	1 − 0 = ☐
4 − 1 = ☐	5 − 1 = ☐	1 − 1 = ☐
5 − 2 = ☐	5 − 4 = ☐	4 − 2 = ☐

Practice with 5-Groups

15	14	13	12	11
10 + 5	10 + 4	10 + 3	10 + 2	10 + 1
	19	18	17	16
	10 + 9	10 + 8	10 + 7	10 + 6

Teen Total Cards

Name _____

VOCABULARY
partners

Write the **partners**.

2

3

3

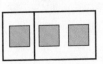

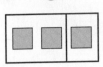

☐ + ☐

☐ + ☐

☐ + ☐

4

4

4

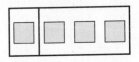

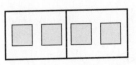

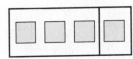

☐ + ☐

☐ + ☐

☐ + ☐

5

5

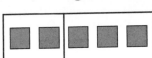

☐ + ☐

☐ + ☐

5

5

☐ + ☐

☐ + ☐

6

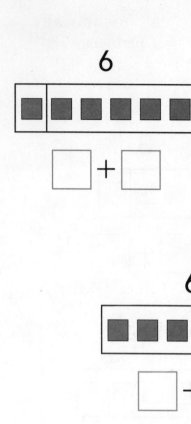

☐ + ☐

6

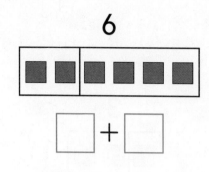

☐ + ☐

6

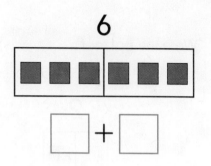

☐ + ☐

6

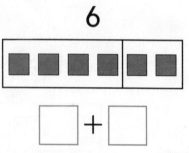

☐ + ☐

6

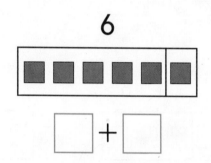

☐ + ☐

7

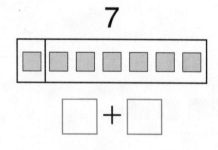

☐ + ☐

7

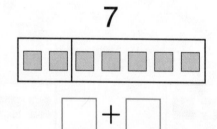

☐ + ☐

7

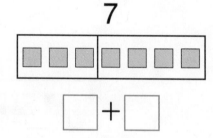

☐ + ☐

7

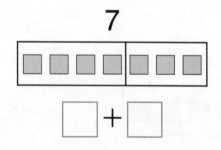

☐ + ☐

7

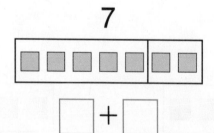

☐ + ☐

7

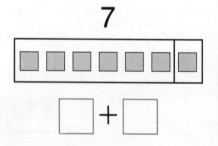

☐ + ☐

Practice with Partners

Dear Family:

In the next few days, please find 20 of the same kind of small object that your child can take to school and paste onto a sheet of paper. For example, your child can use buttons or stickers, or you can cut out 20 small pieces of paper or fabric.

The objects will be used for an activity to help your child learn to see the group of 10 inside each of the teen numbers: 11, 12, 13, 14, 15, 16, 17, 18, and 19.

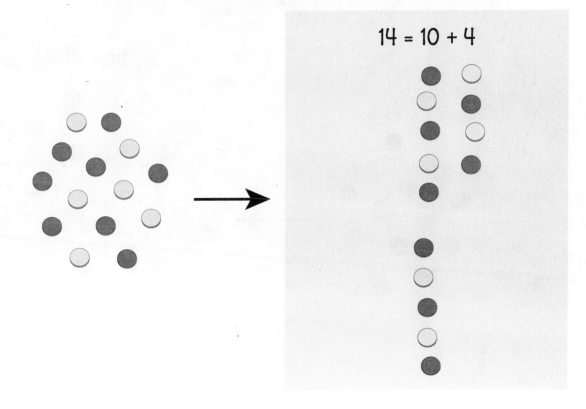

$$14 = 10 + 4$$

Thank you for your cooperation!

Sincerely,
Your child's teacher

COMMON CORE

Unit 3 includes the Common Core Standards for Mathematical Content for Counting and Cardinality K.CC.1, K.CC.2, K.CC.3, K.CC.4, K.CC.4a, K.CC.4b, K.CC.4c, K.CC.5, K.CC.6, K.CC.7; Operations and Algebraic Thinking K.OA.1, K.OA.2, K.OA.3, K.OA.5; Number and Operations in Base Ten K.NBT.1; Measurement and Data K.MD.3; Geometry K.G.1, K.G.2, K.G.4 and all Mathematical Practices.

Estimada familia:

Durante los días siguientes, por favor busque 20 objetos pequeños, del mismo tipo, que su niño pueda llevar a la escuela y pegar en una hoja de papel. Por ejemplo, su niño puede usar botones o adhesivos, o usted puede cortar 20 pedacitos de papel o tela.

Los objetos se usarán en una actividad que ayudará a su niño a identificar el grupo de 10 que hay en cada uno de los números de 11 a 19: 11, 12, 13, 14, 15, 16, 17, 18 y 19.

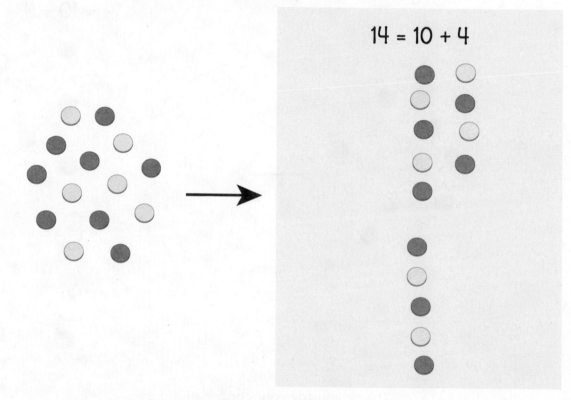

$$14 = 10 + 4$$

¡Gracias por su colaboración!

Atentamente,
El maestro de su niño

La Unidad 3 incluye los Common Core Standards for Mathematical Content for Counting and Cardinality K.CC.1, K.CC.2, K.CC.3, K.CC.4, K.CC.4a, K.CC.4b, K.CC.4c, K.CC.5, K.CC.6, K.CC.7; Operations and Algebraic Thinking K.OA.1, K.OA.2, K.OA.3, K.OA.5; Number and Operations in Base Ten K.NBT.1; Measurement and Data K.MD.3; Geometry K.G.1, K.G.2, K.G.4 and all Mathematical Practices.

Build Teen Numbers with Classroom Objects

VOCABULARY
partners
switched partners

I. Write the **partners**. Look for **switched partners**.

5

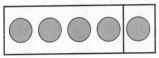

☐ + ☐

5

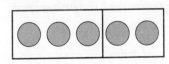

☐ + ☐

5

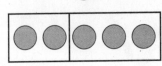

☐ + ☐

6

☐ + ☐

6

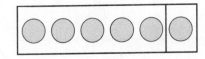

☐ + ☐

6

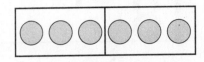

☐ + ☐

7

☐ + ☐

7

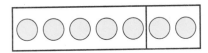

☐ + ☐

7

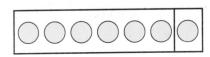

☐ + ☐

5

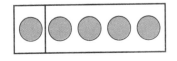

☐ + ☐

6

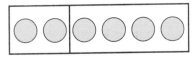

☐ + ☐

7

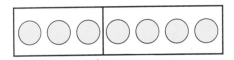

☐ + ☐

2. Write the number 17.

17   17   17   17   17   17

17   17   17   17   17   17

3. Write the number 18.

18   18   18   18   18   18

18   18   18   18   18   18

PATH to FLUENCY

4. Add the numbers.

$0 + 1 = \square$	$0 + 4 = \square$	$3 + 0 = \square$
$1 + 0 = \square$	$1 + 3 = \square$	$4 + 1 = \square$
$3 + 2 = \square$	$2 + 2 = \square$	$2 + 3 = \square$

5. Subtract the numbers.

$3 - 0 = \square$	$2 - 0 = \square$	$5 - 0 = \square$
$3 - 1 = \square$	$5 - 1 = \square$	$2 - 1 = \square$
$5 - 2 = \square$	$5 - 3 = \square$	$4 - 3 = \square$

Build Teen Numbers with Classroom Objects

1. Puzzled Penguin showed the partners
   for two teen numbers and wrote the total.
   Help Puzzled Penguin.

$\underline{12} = 10 + 3 \quad \underline{13} = 10 + 2$

2. Draw the buttons. Write the total.

$\underline{} = 10 + 5 \quad \underline{} = 10 + 1$

3. Write the number 19.

19

19

4. Write the number 20.

20 20 20 20 20

20

PATH to
FLUENCY

5. Add the numbers.

2 + 0 = ☐	0 + 2 = ☐	4 + 0 = ☐
1 + 2 = ☐	0 + 1 = ☐	3 + 1 = ☐
1 + 4 = ☐	5 + 0 = ☐	2 + 3 = ☐

6. Subtract the numbers.

1 − 0 = ☐	4 − 0 = ☐	2 − 0 = ☐
4 − 1 = ☐	1 − 1 = ☐	2 − 1 = ☐
4 − 2 = ☐	5 − 2 = ☐	3 − 2 = ☐

Show Teen Numbers with Classroom Objects

Color all the shapes of one kind the same color.

Count the number of each shape in the picture. Write the number.

Draw your own smiling faces!

_____'s

Robot Family

square	rectangle	circle	triangle	hexagon

Name _____

Circle the picture that matches the statement.

1. The hexagon is **below** the square.

2. The circle is **beside** the triangle.

3. The rectangle is **behind** the triangle.

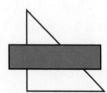 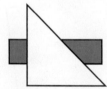

4. The circle is **next to** the square.

Focus on Mathematical Practices

Exercises 1–3. Write the partners.

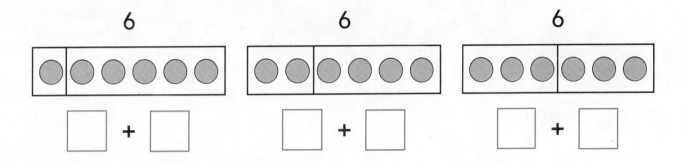

6   6   6

☐ + ☐   ☐ + ☐   ☐ + ☐

Exercise 4. Circle a group of 10. Write how many in all.

Name _____

Exercise 5. Write the number. Draw it using the 5-group.

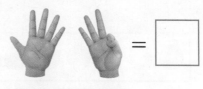 = ☐

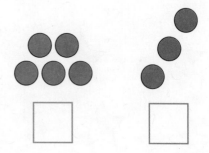

Exercise 6. Write each number and = or ≠.

☐   ☐

Exercise 7. Two triangles are joined.
Draw a line under the new shape they make.

Exercises 8–10. Add the numbers.

4 + 1 = ☐   0 + 2 = ☐   2 + 3 = ☐

Exercises 11–13. Subtract the numbers.

5 – 1 = ☐   4 – 2 = ☐   5 – 3 = ☐

Exercises 14–17. Ring all the triangles.

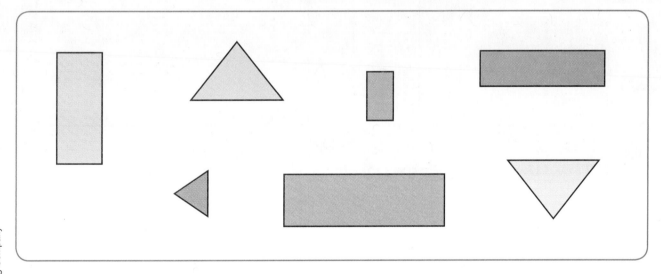

How many triangles are there? ☐

How many rectangles are there? ☐

Ring the shape that has more.

Exercise 18.

Draw 16 using 10 ones and extra ones.

$16 = 10 + 6$

Exercise 19.

Draw a triangle. Draw a circle below it.

Exercise 20. Extended Response Draw to show the problem. Write the answer.

Emma has 5 cards. Max has 2 cards.
How many cards do they have in all?